ARCHITECTURAL DESIGN

GUEST-EDITED BY
MICHAEL HENSEL AND
MEHRAN GHARLEGHI

IRAN
PAST, PRESENT AND FUTURE

03|2012

ARCHITECTURAL DESIGN
MAY/JUNE 2012
ISSN 0003-8504

PROFILE NO 217
ISBN 978-1119-974505

IN THIS ISSUE

ARCHITECTURAL DESIGN

GUEST-EDITED BY
MICHAEL HENSEL AND
MEHRAN GHARLEGHI

IRAN: PAST, PRESENT AND FUTURE

5 EDITORIAL
Helen Castle

6 ABOUT THE GUEST-EDITORS
*Michael Hensel and
Mehran Gharleghi*

8 SPOTLIGHT
Visual highlights of the issue

16 INTRODUCTION
Iran: Past, Present
and Future
*Michael Hensel and
Mehran Gharleghi*

26 Towards an Architectural History of
Performance: Auxiliarity, Performance and
Provision in Historical Persian Architectures
*Michael Hensel, Defne Sunguroğlu Hensel,
Mehran Gharleghi and Salmaan Craig*

38 Persian Gardens and Landscapes
Nasrine Faghih and Amin Sadeghy

EDITORIAL BOARD
Will Alsop
Denise Bratton
Paul Brislin
Mark Burry
André Chaszar
Nigel Coates
Peter Cook
Teddy Cruz
Max Fordham
Massimiliano Fuksas
Edwin Heathcote
Michael Hensel
Anthony Hunt
Charles Jencks
Bob Maxwell
Jayne Merkel
Peter Murray
Mark Robbins
Deborah Saunt
Leon van Schaik
Patrik Schumacher
Neil Spiller
Michael Weinstock
Ken Yeang
Alejandro Zaera-Polo

*What, then, constitutes Iranian sensibilities of the past,
present and future? What are the past traits that merit
rethinking, rearticulating and connecting to relevant
contemporary approaches, and what sort of novel
amalgamation might point towards promising futures
for Iranian architectural design?*
— Michael Hensel

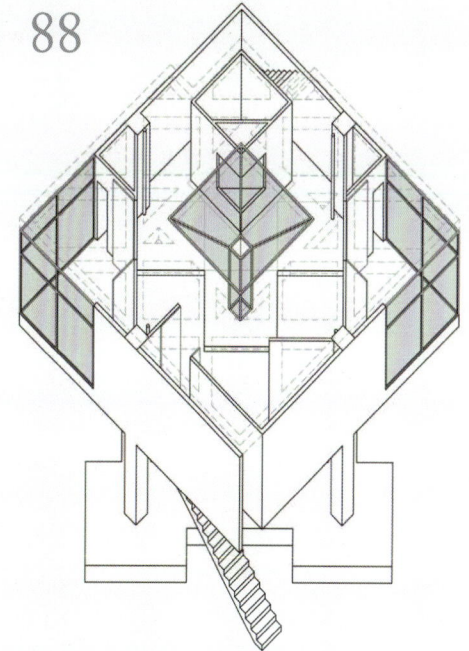

52 World of Similitude:
The Metamorphosis of
Iranian Architecture
Farshad Farahi

62 Subterreanean Landscape:
The Far-Reaching Influence of
the Underground Qanat Network
in Ancient and Present-Day Iran
*Reza Daneshmir and
Catherine Spiridonoff*

70 Contemporary Architecture of Iran
Darab Diba

80 Assimilating the Authentic with
the Contemporary: The Work
of Hadi Mirmiran 1945–2006
Saman Sayar

88 Practices @ Home: Assimilating the
Past and the Present for a
Visionary Architecture
Mehran Gharleghi

104 Practices Abroad: Today's Diaspora
Tomorrow's Architecture
Michael Hensel

Michael Hensel highlights the
work of the Iranian diaspora.
Featuring US-based Hariri &
Hariri and NADAAA, and
London-located Farjadi Architects
and studio INTEGRATE.

120 Latent Futures of Iranian Architecture
Michael Hensel

128 COUNTERPOINT
Iran in the Regional Context
Farrokh Derakhshani

135 CONTRIBUTORS

ARCHITECTURAL DESIGN
MAY/JUNE 2012
PROFILE NO 217

Editorial Offices
John Wiley & Sons
25 John Street
London
WC1N 2BS

T: +44 (0)20 8326 3800

Editor
Helen Castle

Managing Editor (Freelance)
Caroline Ellerby

Production Editor
Elizabeth Gongde

Prepress
Artmedia, London

Art Direction and Design
CHK Design:
Christian Küsters
Sophie Troppmair

Printed in Italy by Conti Tipocolor

Sponsorship/advertising
Faith Pidduck/Wayne Frost
T: +44 (0)1243 770254
E: fpidduck@wiley.co.uk

All Rights Reserved. No part of this publication may be reproduced, stored in a retrieval system or transmitted in any form or by any means, electronic, mechanical, photocopying, recording, scanning or otherwise, except under the terms of the Copyright, Designs and Patents Act 1988 or under the terms of a licence issued by the Copyright Licensing Agency Ltd, 90 Tottenham Court Road, London W1T 4LP, UK, without the permission in writing of the Publisher.

Subscribe to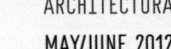

 is published bimonthly and is available to purchase on both a subscription basis and as individual volumes at the following prices.

Prices
Individual copies: £22.99/ US$45
Mailing fees may apply

Annual Subscription Rates
Student: £75 / US$117 print only
Individual: £120 / US$189 print only
Institutional: £200 / US$375 print or online
Institutional: £230 / US$431 combined print and online

Subscription Offices UK
John Wiley & Sons Ltd
Journals Administration Department
1 Oldlands Way, Bognor Regis
West Sussex, PO22 9SA
T: +44 (0)1243 843 272
F: +44 (0)1243 843 232
E: cs-journals@wiley.co.uk

Print ISSN: 0003-8504;
Online ISSN: 1554-2769

Prices are for six issues and include postage and handling charges. Individual rate subscriptions must be paid by personal cheque or credit card. Individual rate subscriptions may not be resold or used as library copies.

All prices are subject to change without notice.

Rights and Permissions
Requests to the Publisher should be addressed to:
Permissions Department
John Wiley & Sons Ltd
The Atrium
Southern Gate
Chichester
West Sussex PO19 8SQ
England

F: +44 (0)1243 770 620
E: permreq@wiley.co.uk

Front cover: studio INTEGRATE with Nasrine Faghih and Archen Consultancy, Saba Naft, Tehran, 2010. © Mehran Gharleghi
Inside front cover: Nazaneen Roxanne Shafaie, Articulated Envelope Experiments, AA Diploma Unit 4 (Michael Hensel and Achim Menges), Architectural Association (AA), London, 2003–4. © Michael Hensel

EDITORIAL
Helen Castle

This title of ⌂ provides a unique opportunity to revisit the rich heritage of Iran, but with an eye sharply focused ahead on its potential for current and future design. The research preoccupations that Michael Hensel and Mehran Gharleghi bring to this issue are substantially different to those that were mined in the 1970s and 1980s when those such as Hassan Fathy ignited a significant interest in vernacular and Islamic architecture in the Middle East. Remarkable historical architectures are studied and researched here from an architectural performance perspective (see pp 26–37). Despite Persia's challenging environment – in terms of terrain and climate – over many centuries it developed sophisticated low-energy or no-energy solutions for structures and its infrastructures. These are perhaps best epitomised by the qanats (subterranean water canals), hydraulic structures that employ gravitational forces to extract and channel groundwater from underground mountain water sources without consuming any energy. What consistently comes through throughout the issue when discussing contemporary Iranian architecture – particularly in Farshad Farahi's and Darab Diba's articles (see pp 52–61 and 70–9), in the description of Hadi Mirmiran's work (see pp 80–7) and that of Iran-based practices (see pp 88–103) – is the way that Iran has sought its own way over the last four decades in developing an architecture that is simultaneously modern and culturally relevant to local traditions. This has developed into a truly original architecture beyond imitation of both Western modern and traditional precedents.

As highlighted so adroitly by Guest-Editors Michael Hensel and Mehran Gharleghi in their introduction, this is also a project that is inspired by the desire to build cultural bridges in an unstable political climate. It is an enterprise that was also embraced by the contributors. As the eminent architect and professor at Tehran University, Darab Diba, expressed to me in an email: 'In the present times of hard social struggles and international sanctions, such coverage concerning our country's cultural activities is very important to present a different aspect of an architecturally active civil society; Iranians who long to have good relations with the world, who look forward to engender international exchanges, and who hate to become so radicalised (and oppressed).' ⌂

Text © 2012 John Wiley & Sons Ltd.
Image © Steve Gorton

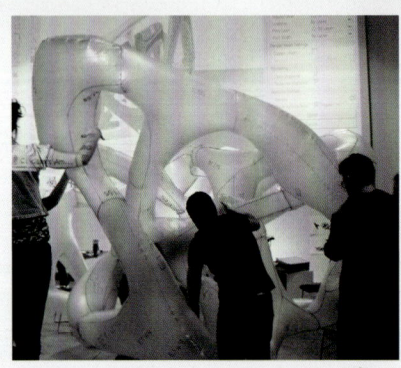

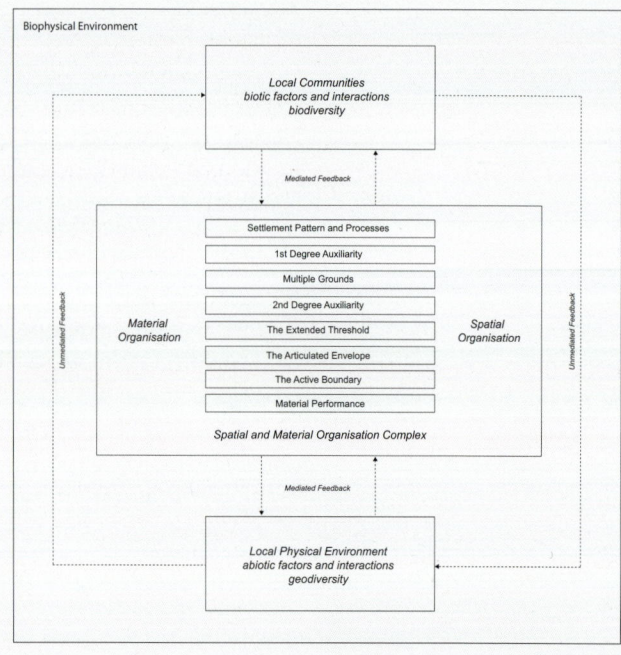

Mehran Gharleghi/studio INTEGRATE, Saba Naft, Tehran, 2010
top left: Saba Naft creates an urban plaza that is covered by a lightweight pneumatic surface. The surface acts as an environmental modulator while allowing a high level of visibility from the office spaces to the surrounding site.

Mehran Gharleghi, Inverscape (draping fabric ceiling), Tina, We Salute You Cafe/Gallery, London, 2011, and Air Bone (pneumatic structure), Graz University of Technology, Graz, Austria, 2011
top right and centre left: The projects show Gharleghi's interest in understanding material's performance to achieve novel geometrical and spatial organisations. Both examples used computational models to predict material's dynamic behaviour and fabrication logic.

Michael Hensel, *Design Innovation for the Built Environment: Research by Design and the Renovation of Practice*, 2012
bottom: Cover of Hensel's latest edited book that surveys the pluralistic field of research by design in architecture.

Michael Hensel, Four Domains of Agency of Performance-Oriented Architecture, 2011
centre right: The diagram shows four domains of agency that underlie Hensel's proposed notion of performance-oriented architecture: (1) local communities (including humans); (2) the local physical environment; (3) the spatial and (4) material organisation complex. By way of adequately mediating the feedback between the biotic and abiotic environments in a nuanced manner, the built environment can be 'in the service of' the natural environment.

ABOUT THE GUEST-EDITORS
MICHAEL HENSEL AND MEHRAN GHARLEGHI

Michael Hensel and Mehran Gharleghi are members of the international and interdisciplinary Sustainable Environment Association (SEA) registered in Norway, and frequently collaborate on research by design efforts.

Michael Hensel is an architect, researcher, educator and writer. He is professor of architecture at the Oslo School of Architecture and Design (AHO) where he directs the Research Center for Architecture and Tectonics (RCAT). He co-founded the OCEAN network in 1994, which became the OCEAN Design Research Association in 2008. He is founding chairman and a board member of the latter. He is also founding chairman and a board member of SEA, a board member of the Biomimetics Network for Industrial Sustainability (BIONIS), and is on the *D* editorial board. His research efforts include the formulation of an integrated theoretical and methodological framework for a non-discrete and non-anthropocentric performance-oriented architecture, rethinking architectural history from a performance perspective, integrating the built and natural environment, and developing research by design efforts in architecture. He has written extensively and taught and lectured worldwide. Forthcoming publications include an *D* Primer on *Performance-Oriented Architecture* and *The Handbook for Traditional Sustainable Buildings* (both being published by John Wiley & Sons).

Mehran Gharleghi is an architect, researcher and educator. He received his BA from Tehran University of Science and Technology (IUST) and his Masters degree from the Emergent Technologies and Design (EmTech) programme at the Architectural Association (AA) in London, where he is now a studio tutor. He is also a studio tutor at the University of Brighton, and has lectured worldwide. He has collaborated with the distinguished Iranian architect Hadi Mirmiran, and also worked for Plasma Studio and Foster + Partners in London. In 2009 he co-founded, with Amin Sadeghy, the studio INTEGRATE international architectural studio based in London. In his work he pursues the synthesis of geometrical, material and fabrication logic with spatial quality, context and culture. His collaborative research with Amin Sadeghy has won numerous awards, including the AA Fab Research Cluster 2009 and the International Prize for Sustainable Architecture 2010. His work was exhibited at the London Design Festival 2009. *D*

Text © 2012 John Wiley & Sons Ltd. Images: pp 6(t), 7(b) © Mehran Gharleghi; pp 6(br), 7(t) © Michael Hensel

SPOTLIGHT

NADAAA/Office dA with Johnston Marklee and Big

Helios House Gas Station, Los Angeles, 2007
The expressive sculptural character of the gas station is in stark contrast to its nondescript urban context.

Pouya Khazaeli Parsa

Bamboo Structure, Mazandaran, Iran, 2009
Experimental structure using bamboo in an innovative way to synthesise material characteristics and fabrication logic and to accommodate the complex geometry. The choice of material is informed by the vernacular architecture of Northern Iran.

studio INTEGRATE with Nasrine Faghih + Archen Consultancy

Saba Naft, Tehran, 2010
Like the Benetton scheme opposite, this project features two distinct parts of the building envelope: a more straight-lined opaque and framing one, and a curvilinear and geometrically highly articulated one. However, while the Benetton scheme is more introverted, Saba Naft is explicitly extrovert, using its massing to orient the interior towards or away from climatic influences. Rendered view.

Benetton Headquarters, Tehran, 2009
The articulation of the building volume in this proposal suggests an image of the dissection of geological mass by a tight canyon with a crystalline surface, or an Islamic vault violently distorted by the rotational movement of a cyclone. The geometrically highly articulated inner surface and the veiling outer one generate a heterogeneous field of material effects, while the tight 'courtyard' space enables passive environmental modulation.

Hadi Mirmiran

National Library of Iran, Tehran, 1995
The glazed roof rises from the ground level creating a fifth facade for the building.

For me, in the beginning of the design process the most important thing is finding the 'design's turning point' of the project. It means, knowing what the origin of the design is ... sometimes it is a form, or a concept, a poem, or a memory, sometimes it is a dream, a myth, or an idea.
— *Hadi Mirmiran, 1999*

Text © 2012 John Wiley & Sons Ltd. Images: pp 8–9 © NADAAA/Office dA, photo Eric Staudenmaier; pp 10–11 © Pouya Khazeli Parsa; pp 12–13 © studio INTEGRATE; pp 14–15 © Hamid Mirmiran, Naqsh-e-Jahan-Pars (NJP) consulting engineers

Come in through the door of exaltation, And do not seek the faults of others.

—Poem from *The Diwan* of Hafiz Shirazi[1]

INTRODUCTION
By Michael Hensel and Mehran Gharleghi

IRAN

PAST, PRESENT AND FUTURE

Why *Iran: Past, Present and Future*? Two sincere intentions underlie this effort: first, to introduce the past and present architectures of a place that witnessed the unfolding of one of the most astonishing high cultures of human history; and second, to make a succinct attempt to build cultural bridges towards a better future across deep-seated divides.

The West-Eastern Divan Orchestra, a project conceived by the late Palestinian–American literary theorist Edward Said and the Argentine–Israeli conductor Daniel Barenboim, was an inspiration for the overarching intent of this title and a previous issue of △ entitled *Turkey: At the Threshold* (Jan/Feb 2010) guest-edited by Hülya Ertaş, Michael Hensel and Defne Sunguroğlu Hensel. Founded in 1999 and based in Seville in Spain, the West-Eastern Divan Orchestra consists of musicians from Egypt, Iran, Israel, Jordan, Lebanon, Palestine, Syria and Spain who perform together irrespective of past and present political, religious and armed conflicts. Barenboim stated that 'the Divan was conceived as a project against ignorance', to 'create the conditions for understanding' and to 'awaken the curiosity of each individual to listen to the narrative of the other'. Moreover, he argued that 'acceptance of the freedom

Qanats
opposite: Aerial photo of Kashan in Iran showing the traces of underground water canals, so-called qanats, in the surface of the landscape.

above: A qanat terminating in a pool in Sole, Soleimanieh, Iran.

17

Isfahan Bridges
left: Khaju Bridge (*pol-e khajoo*), c 1650.

right: Bridge of 33 Arches (*si-o-se pol*), c 1600.

Khaju Bridge (*pol-e khajoo*), Isfahan, Iran, c 1650
opposite centre: Computer fluid dynamics (CFD) analysis showing airflow through the bridge.

opposite bottom: Solar analysis showing the shaded areas of the two-level bridge.

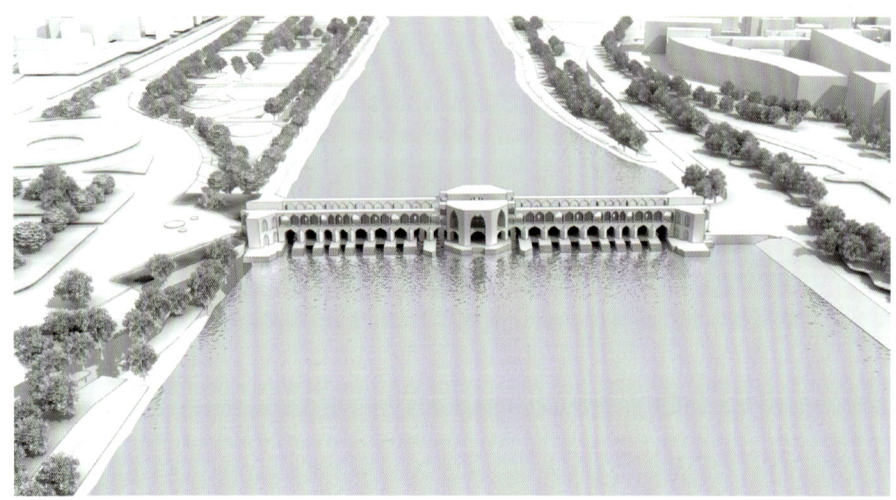

and individuality of the other is one of music's most important lessons'.[2]

And so one begins to wonder whether architecture too could contribute in such a marvellous manner. Can it create curiosity, communication and acceptance across troubled divides? Whether one believes so or not, it is entirely worth the effort. At this very moment in time, conflict is flaring up again at an alarming rate in the Middle East and cultural bridges are in dire need where destructive forces hold sway. The Arab Spring fuels great hopes and deep-seated worries alike, as nobody knows in which direction the pendulum might swing. Perhaps, when all cultures and ethnic groups are adequately recognised and given the opportunity to express themselves, and are met with sincere interest, the readiness for conflict may fade. Additionally, given the current cultural, environmental and economic crises in general, and in the discipline of architecture in particular, it would seem obvious that the latter can only gain by seeking to operate once again as both platform and object of cultural discourse and intensified exchange.

This issue looks beyond the geographical and political borders of the Islamic Republic of Iran both in space and in time. As the cradle and home of one of the oldest high cultures,

Iran has been a heterogeneous sphere of changing geographic extent and cultural and ethnical mix. From the pre-Islamic (625 BC–AD 651) Medes, Achaemenid, Seleucid, Parthian and Sassanid empires, to the Middle Age (652–1501) Abbasid, Tahirid, Saffarid, Samanid, Ziyarid, Buyid, Ghaznavid, Seljuk and Khwarazm dynasties, to the Early Modern era (1501–1925) Safavid, Afsharid, Zand, Qajar and Pahlavi dynasties and the Islamic Republic (1979–), the extent and alliances of the country have varied greatly. The ancient Persian Royal Road rebuilt and extended under Darius I in the 5th century BC facilitated rapid communication and coincided in parts with the Silk Road and thus long-distance trade for centuries to come. It also enabled cultural exchange at an accelerated rate.

Throughout Persia, history, philosophy, poetry, the arts, mathematics, physics, astronomy, medicine, biology, chemistry, technology, architecture and craftsmanship flourished to incredible heights of sophistication. The names of many brilliant polymaths shine through the ages: Abu Ali al-Husayn ibn Abd Allah ibn Sina known to the occident as Avicenna (c 980–1037), Omar Khayyám (1048–1131) and Nasir al-Din al-Tusi (1201–74). Further extraordinary heights were reached during the Safavid

era under Shah Abbas I and Shah Abbas II in the 16th and 17th centuries. Often, as in the latter cases, new developments were triggered by the confluence of different vernacular and architectural traditions of different regions of the empire and beyond, enabling design that clearly leapt forward in its innovativeness, and in the process fostering what might be seen as time-specific Iranian sensibilities.

Today, Iran's ethnically diverse population is estimated at above 75 million people.

In addition, the country currently hosts around a million refugees from Afghanistan and Iraq. Estimates of the size of the Iranian diaspora vary greatly between one and four million. And so one begins to wonder whether the remarkable sophistication of architectures past has been continued in some way, or whether it has been considerably transformed, diminished or altogether relinquished in the wake of a more globalised approach. Has its history of remarkably integrated expression and functionality made it resilient to trends of globalisation, or has it been swiped away without trace like elsewhere? Are there one or several discernible traits that characterise Iranian architecture today, and if so what sets them apart from other architectures? Is the work of the Iranian architectural diaspora

Plans, axonometrics, elevations and axonometric sections of the selected historical case studies in the issue
below: From left to right: The Meybod ice house in the Yazd region, Pigeon Tower in Isfahan, Boroujerdi's House in Kashan and the Khaju Bridge in Isfahan.

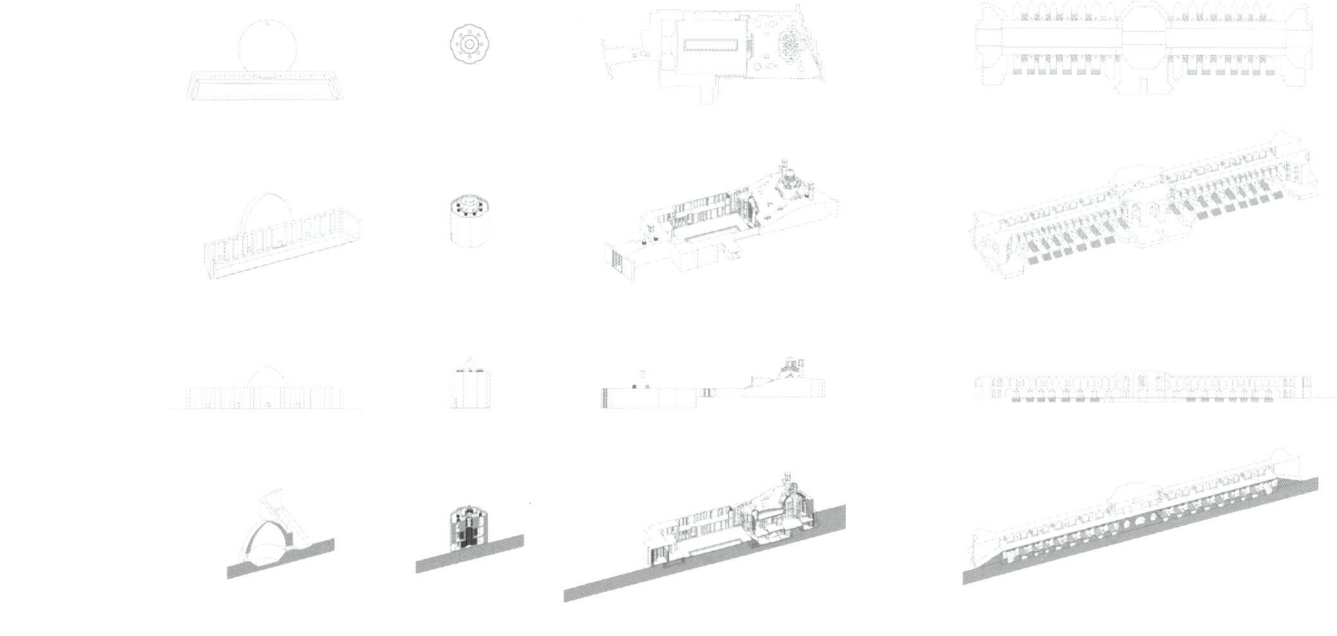

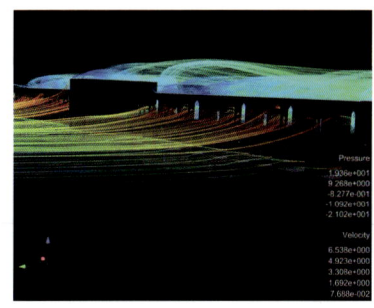

similar or different to that of architects located in Iran? What can similarities and dissimilarities tell us about the impact of context? And what can be learned from a first glimpse at Iran's past, present and future architectures?

In search of answers to these questions, this issue of ⌂ seeks to connect a number of thought-provoking aspects of historical and contemporary Iranian architecture. The effort commences with two articles that focus on remarkable historical architectures from an architectural performance perspective.[3] This includes specifically works from the Safavid period (1501–1736), in particular under Shah Abbas I (1571–1629)[4] and Shah Abbas II (1632–66), as well as selected later works. Michael Hensel, Defne Sunguroğlu Hensel, Mehran Gharleghi and Salmaan Craig's article 'Towards an Architectural History of Performance: Auxiliarity, Performance and Provision in Historical Persian Architectures' (pp 27–37) examines the Khaju Bridge (*pol-e khajoo*) (c 1650) and pigeon towers in Isfahan, an ice house in the Yazd region, as well as a water reservoir (1630) and the Boroujerdi's House (1857) located in Kashan. Subsequently, Dr Nasrine Faghih and Amin Sadeghy focus on the Fin Garden and kiosk (1629) built in its present form under

World of Similitude
below and opposite: The strong presence of water in Iranian architecture.

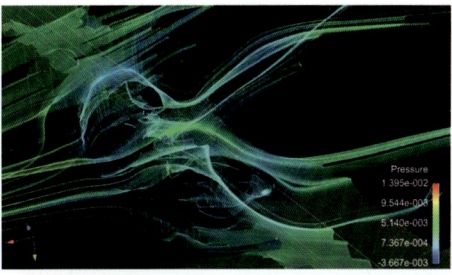

Fin Garden, Kashan, Isfahan, Iran, 1629
left: CFD analysis showing the airflow through the Fin Kiosk.

below: Views of the Fin Garden kiosk showing its setting within the dense vegetation of the garden, as well as its heterogeneous exterior–interior relation.

Hadi Mirmiran, Rafsanjan Sport Complex, Rafsanjan, Iran, 2002
Mirmiran referred to the form of historical ice houses in the design of the swimming pool for the Rafsanjan Sport Complex.

Hadi Mirmiran, National Academies of the Islamic Republic of Iran, Tehran, 1994
Here, elements from historical Iranian architecture, such as the platform, central courtyard and dome are masterfully composed.

Hadi Mirmiran, Embassy of Iran in Bangkok, Bangkok, 2006
The Embassy design follows that of traditional Persian gardens.

the reign of Shah Abbas I in Kashan (see pp 38–51). These articles seek to examine potentials in projects that have not lost any of their relevance and can thus help to re-inform architectural practice in the region today, and that in similar climate zones.

This is followed by Farshad Farahi's article 'World of Similitude: The Metamorphosis of Iranian Architecture' (pp 52–61), which focuses on the development from historical to contemporary Iranian architecture. Reza Daneshmir and Catherine Spiridonoff's article 'Subterranean Landscape: The Far-Reaching Influence of the Underground Qanat Network in Ancient and Present-Day Iran' (pp 62–9) discusses the potential of the historical qanat network for underground water distribution as an alternative means for contemporary urban design that can collaborate with other urban systems. Professor Darab Diba's 'Contemporary Architecture of Iran' (pp 70–9) looks at significant influences on the different stages of the development of current Iranian architecture.

Subsequently, Saman Sayar outlines the distinguished works of the influential architect Hadi Mirmiran (1945–2006) and introduces a number of projects built in and outside of Iran.

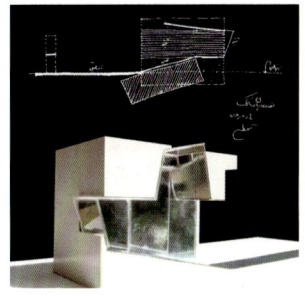

Pouya Khazaeli Parsa, Bamboo Structure, Mazandaran, Iran, 2009
left: Commonly used vernacular materials have here been used to achieve a complex geometrical organisation.

Arsh Design Studio, Dollat I, Tehran, 2005, and Dollat II, Tehran, 2007
centre: Arsh Design Studio has attempted to raise the standard of Iran's traditional four- and five-storey apartment buildings.

Kourosh Rafiey, Parchin Residential Building, Anzali, Iran, 2009, and Amaj Darman, Pardis Technology Park, Tehran, 2009
right and below: Rafiey adapts his design method to suit the specifics and location of each of his projects.

NADAAA (formerly Office dA), Banq, Boston, Massachusetts, 2008
opposite top: Top row, left: Flat sheet materials create a dynamic free form.

Nader Tehrani, Student Research Project at Georgia Institute of Technology, Atlanta, Georgia, 2006
opposite top: Top row, centre left: NADAAA works across a wide range of scales from products and furniture to large-scale buildings and urban design.

Fluid Motion Architects (FMA), Mellat Park Cineplex, Tehran, 2008
The connection of the two sloped faces of the cineplex serves as a huge public platform.

'Practices @ Home' (pp 88–103) introduces a number of offices that practice in Iran, including Fluid Motion Architects (FMA), Arsh Design Studio, Kourosh Rafiey (Asar Consultant Engineers' Co) and Pouya Khazaeli Parsa. 'Practices Abroad: Today's Diaspora Tomorrow's Architecture' (pp 104–19) focuses on Iranian practices outside of Iran, including Hariri & Hariri in New York, NADAAA (formerly Office dA) in Boston, Massachusetts, and Farjadi Architects and studio INTEGRATE in London in search of existing or latent Iranian sensibilities in contemporary Iranian architecture. The penultimate article, 'The Latent Futures of Iranian Architecture' by Michael Hensel (pp 120–27) offers some reflections on noteworthy questions and trajectories as to the future of Iranian architecture, in as far as such an entity might continue to exist. The issue concludes with the 'Counterpoint' offered by Farrokh Derakhshani, Director of the Aga Khan Award for Architecture (see pp 128–34).

In trying to follow the extraordinary example of the West-Eastern Divan Orchestra, the Sustainable Environment Association (SEA) was founded in 2011 to bring together experts from the disciplines of architecture, urban design, anthropology, environmental engineering, climatology and microclimatology, biological ecology and urban ecology and a wide variety of national and ethnic backgrounds to collaborate on questions concerning the relationship between the human-dominated and built environment on the one hand, and the natural environment on the other. The late Hassan Fathy elucidated that:

> [The architect] must renew architecture from the moment when it was abandoned; and he must try to bridge the existing gap in its development by analyzing the elements of change, applying modern techniques to modify the valid methods established by our ancestors, and then developing new solutions that satisfy modern needs.[5]

It is in the context of this understanding that the SEA interrelates questions regarding performance-oriented architecture, building traditions, craftsmanship, scientific and technological advancements, and biotic and abiotic environments in search of integrated complex approaches to architectural design and sustainability. The titles of 𝔇 on Iran and Turkey feature in various articles the first analyses focused on historical Persian and Ottoman architectures. This is significant when considering the frequent historical

studio INTEGRATE, Air Bone, Graz University of Technology, Graz, Austria, 2011
Top row, centre right: Complex computational and physical methods are synthesised to extend the geometrical and fabrication possibilities of pneumatic material systems.

studio INTEGRATE, Inverscape, Tina, We Salute You Cafe/Gallery, London, 2011
Top row, right: The dynamic behaviour of non-stretchable draping fabrics was anticipated digitally and fabricated through the integration of digital and physical techniques.

NADAAA (formerly Office dA) with Johnston Marklee and Big, Helios House Gas Station, Los Angeles, 2007
Bottom row, left: The functional requirements of the house dictate its free-form architecture.

NADAAA (formerly Office dA), Tongxian Art Gatehouse, Beijing, 2003
Bottom row, centre left: The design of the Tongxian Art Gatehouse demonstrates NADAAA's non-standard approach to using standard elements such as brick.

studio INTEGRATE, Benetton Headquarters, Tehran, 2009
Bottom row, centre right: Penrose geometries have been used to articulate a complex geometrical organisation from only a few basic geometrical modules.

studio INTEGRATE with Nasrine Faghih and Archen Consultancy, Saba Naft, Tehran, 2010
Bottom row, right: Saba Naft focuses on the integration of geometric complexity, spatial organisation, material effect and environmental conditioning.

conflicts between the Ottoman and Persian empires and current developments in the Middle East. Now is the time to step away from prevailing political presumptions and their negative repercussions and to concentrate instead on sustainable cultural, environmental and economic collaboration. In so doing, cultural specificity can become the focus of mutual interest and gain. The ⌂ issues on Iran and Turkey are intended as part of such an effort. In this way perhaps architecture may be able to provide an equivalent opportunity to the one epitomised by the West-Eastern Divan Orchestra. ⌂

Fluid Motion Architects, Safaeie Multifunctional Complex, Yazd, 2010
The spatial organisation of traditional architecture in dry climates such as Yazd has been applied in this modern complex.

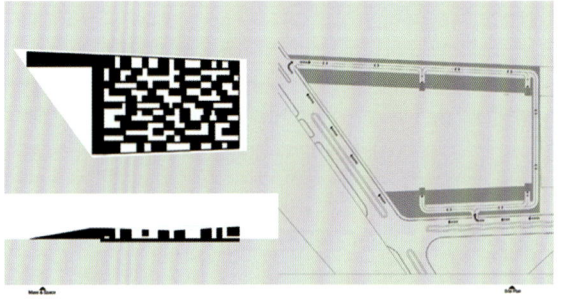

Fluid Motion Architects, Vali-Asr-Mosque, Tehran, due for completion 2013
left and bottom: The mosque has created an urban plaza adjacent to the landmark City Theatre.

Farjadi Architects and Turenscape China, Suzhou Park Development, Jiangsu, China, 2011
top: The landscaped surface and concourse spaces at Suzhou Park are a recurring theme in the collaborative work of Farjadi Architects and Turenscape China.

  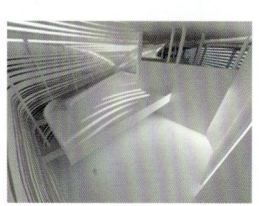 

[The architect] must renew architecture from the moment when it was abandoned; and he must try to bridge the existing gap in its development by analyzing the elements of change, applying modern techniques to modify the valid methods established by our ancestors, and then developing new solutions that satisfy modern needs.
— *Hassan Fathy, 1986*

Hariri & Hariri, Belmont House, San Francisco, 2002
The Belmont project explores the fusion between two of the region's popular vernacular architectures: the mobile trailer home and he Mexican pueblo.

Notes
1. From AJ Alston, *In Search of Hafiz: 109 Poems from the Diwan*, trans AJ Alston, Shanti Sadan (London), 1996, p 487.
2. E Vulliamy, 'Bridging the Gap – Part Two', *The Observer*, 13 July 2008.
See: www.guardian.co.uk/music/2008/jul/13/classicalmusicandopera. culture (accessed 12 August 2011).
3. More detailed studies of the selected buildings will be included in the forthcoming *Handbook of Sustainable Traditional Architecture* by the Sustainable Environment Association (SEA) to be published by John Wiley & Sons in 2013.
4. In 2009, the British Museum had mounted an astonishing exhibition on Shah Abbas's reign entitled 'Shah Abbas – The Remaking of Iran'. A wonderfully illustrated catalogue accompanied this exhibition: SR Canby, *Shah Abbas – The Remaking of Iran*, The British Museum Press (London), 2009.
5. H Fathy, *Natural Energy and Vernacular Architecture: Principles and Examples with Relevance to Hot Arid Climates*, University of Chicago Press (Chicago, IL), 1986, p xxiii.

Text © 2012 John Wiley & Sons Ltd. Images: pp 16–17, 21(tl&ct) © Hamidreza Jayhani; p 18 © Dr Sepehri, photos by Jassem Ghazbanpour; pp 19, 21(tr) © SEA – Sustainable Environment Association: Michael Hensel, Mehran Gharleghi, Amin Sadeghy; p 20 © Fattaneh Dadkhan; p 21(cb&b) © Hamid Mirmiran, Naqsh-e-Jahan-Pars (NJP) consulting engineers; p 22(tl) © Pouya Khazeli Parsa; p 22(tc) Arsh Design Studio; p 22(tr&c) © Kourosh Rafiey; pp 22(b), 23(b), 24(b) © Reza Daneshmir/Fluid Motion Architects; p 23(t) © NADAAA/Office dA and studio INTEGRATE; p 24(t) © Farjadi Architects & Turenscape; p 25 © Hariri & Hariri Architecture

Acknowledgements
This work would not have been possible without the dedicated and coordinated effort of many. We would like to offer our sincere gratitude to: our friends for their unwavering support and collaboration, in particular Amin Sadeghy and Tomasz Mlynarski; all the contributors to this issue of ⌂; Dr Nasrine Faghih and Professor Hamidreza Sepehri, General Director of the Architecture and Urban Research Center of Iran for helping with sponsorship and providing valuable documentation of the historical cases; the Isfahan Cultural Heritage Organization for providing valuable documentation; the Mirmiran Architecture Foundation, Hamid Mirmiran, Managing Director of Naqsh-e-Jahan-Pars (NJP) consulting engineers, for providing valuable documents; Pouya Khazeli Parsa for providing resources and the help of his students; Matthew Foreman (Foster + Partners), Mahsa Ramezanpour, Maryam Mahdieh, Mehrnoush Bajoghli, Mahmood Rezaei, Hasan Azad and Mohammad Ali Mirzaie for research and document collection; Ashkan Sadeghi, Yasaman Mousavi, Fatemeh Naseri for 3D modelling; Harsh Thapar for environmental and CFD consultancy; Aidan Doyle for copy-editing; the OCEAN Design Research Association and the Research Centre for Architecture and Tectonics at the Oslo School of Architecture and Design for resources, in particular rapid prototyping; Computational Engineering International (CEI) for temporary licences of EnSight®, and the ThermoAnalytics Incorporation (TAI) for temporary licences of RadTherm®; and finally, Helen Castle for her immense support and constructive input throughout the production of this issue, and the ⌂ team, particularly Caroline Ellerby and Christian Küsters for their thorough and committed work.

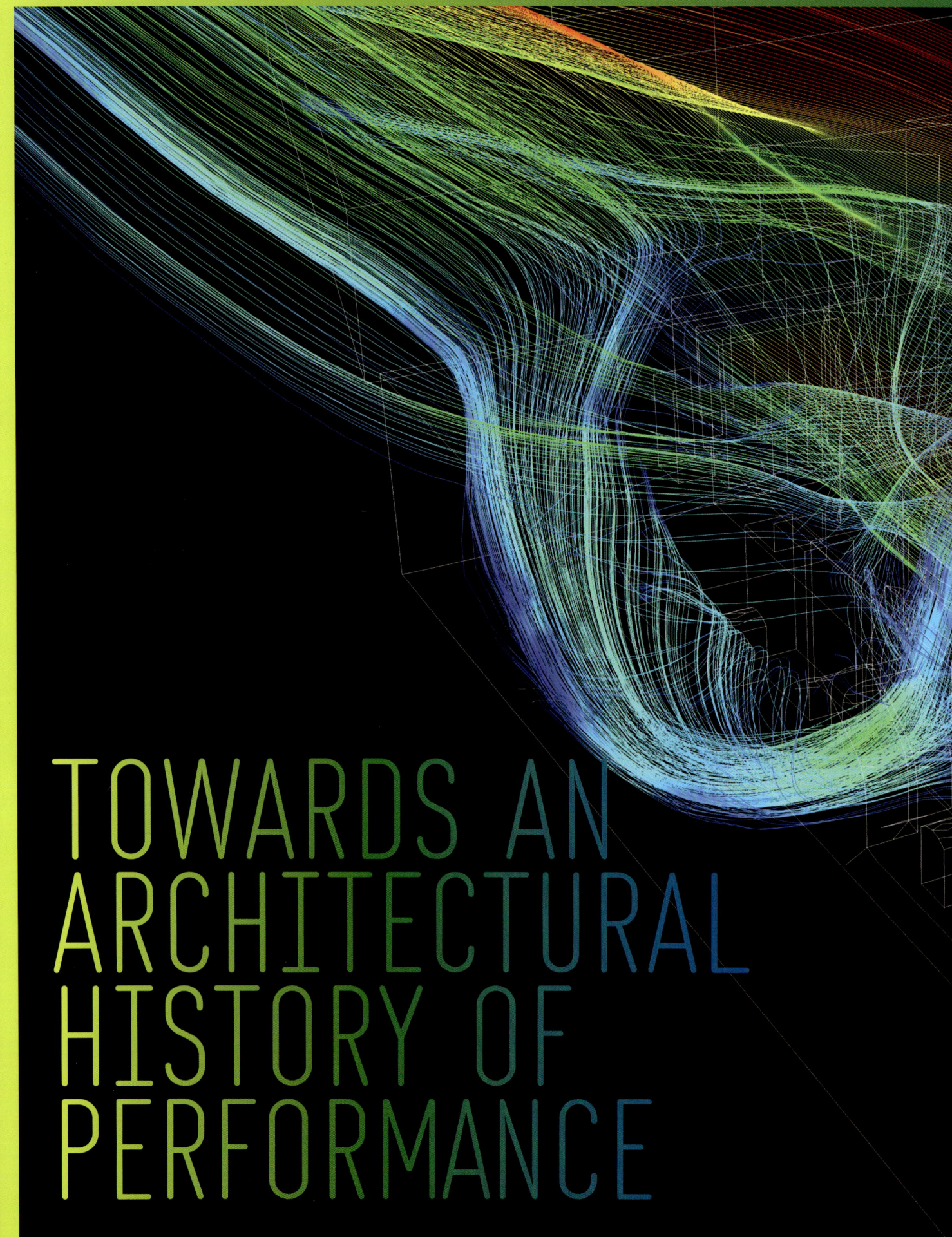

*Michael Hensel, Defne Sunguroğlu Hensel,
Mehran Gharleghi and Salmaan Craig*

AUXILIARITY, PERFORMANCE AND PROVISION IN HISTORICAL PERSIAN ARCHITECTURES

Despite its extensive empire, Persia historically presented a challenging environment for the building of structures and infrastructure. The mountainous landscape of the Iranian plateau has an arid or semi-arid climate with distinct seasonal variations and temperatures that fluctuate throughout the day. Despite this, water management and soil-fertilisation strategies and passive environmental modulation in architecture were all highly developed previous to the 19th century so as to be finely attuned to the local context, while also responding to the greater demands of a centralised empire. Here **Michael Hensel, Defne Sunguroğlu Hensel, Mehran Gharleghi and Salmaan Craig** discuss and illustrate their detailed findings of the performance of historic structures. These include qanats (water canals), water cisterns, ice houses and pigeon houses as well as the seminal Khaju Bridge in Isfahan and the Boroujerdi's House in Kashan.

The clouds, the wind, the moon, and the sun,
For your comfort, and at your behest run.
They toil continuously for your satisfaction,
Should you not halt, monitor your action?
— Sheikh Muslih-uddin Sa'di Shirazi,
Prologue to the Gulistan (or Rose Garden), 1258[1]

The distinguished German architect Frei Otto described an obvious, significant and often overlooked trait of architecture when he stated that 'constructions are auxiliary means, not an end in themselves'.[2] 'Auxiliarity' implies intentional and cohesive relations beyond the physical limits of a construction that embed it intensively into a larger dynamic context. As an example, Otto specified that a bridge is auxiliary to the road system of which it is part. Yet architectures can be simultaneously auxiliary to several systems including conditions that are not man-made. The eminent American architectural scholar David Leatherbarrow elaborated that architecture always 'participates in numerous authored and un-authored conditions'.[3] This includes, for example, the interaction of constructions with the local climate and the resulting production of a microclimate, and suggests that if 'participation' and its consequences are not thought-through the resulting conditions will be accidental and possibly unsuitable. The difference between Otto's notion of auxiliarity and Leatherbarrow's notion of 'participation' rests, therefore, in the fact that the former entails intentional functional relations, while the latter takes place whether considered by the architect or not.

Consequently, the realisation arises that the extent to which architectures are auxiliary to all sorts of conditions, as well as the kind and degree of their participation, can be made a central concern of architectural design and the means by which architecture enacts and expands its repertoire of making provisions for habitation. These provisions may cater for humans or other species, potentially even entire agro- or ecosystems, and can help to sustain local economies, depending on the auxiliary relations and resulting conditions that are involved. Moreover, the combined relations between auxiliarity, participation and projected provision are traits of an alternative approach to sustainability that resonates with the specific take of Paul Reitan, Professor Emeritus of Geological Sciences at the University of Buffalo:

> Successfully sustainable human societies must ... be as attuned as possible to their local and regional environments, their geo-ecological support systems; lifestyles must be adapted to the ecosystems in which societies live and which support them with cultures, practices, economic systems, and governing policies each adjusted to fit their area, not a single dominant culture or way of living spread across the globe. This would be a world of multiple, diverse societies with their numbers also adjusted to what regional geo-ecological support systems can sustain.[4]

This understanding would have seemed entirely obvious to ancient Persian 'planners' and masterbuilders. The particular environmental challenges faced by the Persian builders included the largely arid or semi-arid climate of the mountainous landscape of the Iranian plateau with distinct seasonal differences and steep seasonal and daily temperature gradients. Context-specific water management and soil-fertilisation strategies, passive environmental modulation in architecture and related settlement pattern were all finely attuned to the context. The size of the country also posed a challenge. At 1.648 million square kilometres (636,296 square miles), today Iran is the eighteenth largest country in the world. Yet throughout its history the Persian Empire was often considerably larger. Thus the development of massive infrastructure and refined local architectures took place concomitantly, and auxiliarity was a self-evident requisite. The associated development and exchange of knowledge and skills is embedded in whatever is left of the historical built environment, and is worth examining for knowledge that can be updated and put to task today.

During the time of the Achaemenid, or first Persian Empire (c 550–300 BC), the so-called Persian Royal Road connected vast stretches of the empire. It is thought that the Assyrians built the oldest part of this road, but it was substantially reorganised and extended into the Royal Road under Darius I (c 550–486 BC). Its purpose was to facilitate fast communication and post via couriers, and long-distance trade, and it coincided in parts with the Silk Routes, a network of land and water trade routes that connected Asia with Europe and North and East Africa, with the Persian Empire located at the centre. Along these routes, not only goods, but also knowledge, was conveyed. Roads, bridges, post stations, caravanserais, water reservoirs and other types of constructions facilitated this efficient system in a locally specific manner and were improved upon through the exchanges facilitated by the routes network. There was thus no conflict between 'global' and 'local' aspects. On the contrary, it can be clearly discerned that the exchange of knowledge led to major improvements in the locally specific built environment of the Persian plateau and other parts of the Persian Empire. In particular during the Safavid era under Shah Abbas I (Shah Abbas the Great) (1571–1629) and later Shah Abbas II (1632–66), new heights of refinement and complexity of architectures were reached. Recently experts have begun to emphasise the remarkable impact of the multi-ethnic and multi-religious population of Isfahan under the rule of Shah Abbas I on the remaking of the city and its architecture, when the shah pronounced Isfahan the new imperial capital in 1598. Dr Emma Loosley pointed out that 'a variety of communities lived and worked alongside each other' and that 'Abbas was ahead of his time in discerning the practical and economic value of a multicultural society'.[5] The accumulative effect of this coexistence and the already rich history of architecture led to an abundance of civic, representational, vernacular and special-purpose architectures that were characterised by a high level of integrated functional capacity and formal expression.

Designing Flows: Qanats and *badgirs*

Many architectures of historical Persia display the masterly deployment of the flow of water and air to provide a habitable environment. In the case of water it often had to be brought from afar, stored and distributed. In the case of airflow, the purpose was passive ventilation and thermal conditioning. In numerous examples the flows were correlated in an advantageous manner, and the outcomes were invariably immensely well-calibrated constructions and architectures of stunning beauty and performance. Two key elements were a water management system (qanat) and the wind towers (*badgir* and *khishkhan*).

In ancient Persia rivers were sparse and often seasonal. This made alternative methods of water management an indispensable necessity to provide continuous irrigation for agricultural purposes and drinking water for settlements in the largely arid regions of Persia. The combination of fertile soil and precipitation-rich mountain ranges made it viable to collect groundwater at the foot of the mountains with a system of subterranean canals called qanats. The oldest existing qanats in Iran date from around 1000 BC. It is generally thought that this system was developed in Persia and that it was gradually diffused from here westwards to the arid zones of Mediterranean North Africa, Italy and Spain, and eastwards to Afghanistan, Pakistan and Turfan in Northwest China. The most extensive qanats found to date are up to 70 kilometres (43.5 miles) long and located in the Kerman region. On average, however, qanats were about 5 to 10 kilometres (3 to 6 miles) long. The exactitude of the slope of the qanat was of vital importance to prevent destructive flow conditions or stagnation. Qanats feature vertical shafts at an interval of on average of 25 metres (82 feet), which are necessary both for the construction and the ventilation of the system. Their subterranean location made it possible to avoid extensive evaporative water loss, contamination of the water, as well as substantial damage through floods and earthquakes. A system of smaller channels (*kariz*) enabled the distribution of water from the qanats to water cisterns of individual buildings, and so on. Appointed individuals (*meerab*) were responsible for the operation of the *kariz* and the filling of the water cisterns. Maintenance was crucial as qanats, *kariz* and water cisterns needed to be periodically cleaned due to sediments.

Wind towers (*badgir* and *khishkhan*) were an integral part of a series of interrelated strategies for passive building climatisation in the hot and arid regions of Iran that are characterised by a steep day-to-night temperature gradient. Settlements are typically arranged in a dense manner to minimise thermal impact. Buildings are constructed from adobe bricks and walls are very thick to gain high capacity for thermal regulation and heat transmission resistance. The *badgir*-type wind towers are chimney-like structures that serve the purpose of passive ventilation and interior climatisation. The orientation of openings at the exposed upper part of the wind tower and the arrangement of the vertical air ducts and dividing blades inside is directly related to various types of functions and local conditions.[6] Mehdi Bahadori elucidated that wind towers 'differ in the height of the tower, the cross-section of the air passages, the placement and number of openings and the placement of the tower with respect to the structure it cools'.[7]

Many architectures of historical Persia display the masterly deployment of the flow of water and air to provide a habitable environment. In the case of water it often had to be brought from afar, stored and distributed. In the case of airflow, the purpose was passive ventilation and thermal conditioning.

Through simple shutters, different air ducts inside the wind tower could be closed to change its function from mono-directional to bidirectional or multidirectional, depending on the required use. Bahadori explained that:

> the operation of the tower depends on wind conditions and the time of day ... when there is no wind at night the tower operates like a chimney, circulating air by pulling it upward and through the tower openings ... when there is a wind at night, the air is forced in the opposite direction; the rooms are cooled by night air coming down the tower ... when there is no wind during the day, the operation of the tower is the reverse of a chimney. The walls of the upper part of the tower have been cooled during the previous night. Hot air comes in contact with them and is cooled. Being denser than the hot air, the cooled air sinks down through the tower, creating a downdraft ... when there is a wind during the day, the rate of circulation is increased.[8]

This short excerpt from Bahadori's detailed report begins to show just how versatile the use of the wind towers can be. This can be enhanced when the airflow is combined with a fountain or water basin to achieve additional evaporative cooling. Windcatchers were also frequently used in combination with a qanat. In this case a mono-directional arrangement with leeward-facing opening of the windcatcher made use of the pressure differential to draw out air from the building. An air channel external to the building served as an inlet through which air was drawn downwards to an underground qanat and chilled through evaporative cooling. This cooled air was then drawn into the basement and other parts of the house.

The *khishkhan*-type wind tower is a dome with an opening placed on the roof of buildings that enabled both ventilation and indirect light into the space below – typically the main hall or living room. It could also be used for evaporative cooling, covered with a wooden mesh, clay, or dried plants and moistened in order to cool the air flowing into the building.[9]

Sophisticated historical Persian architectures typically combine numerous strategies for the production of suitable microclimates for a variety of purposes, as can be seen from the selected examples.

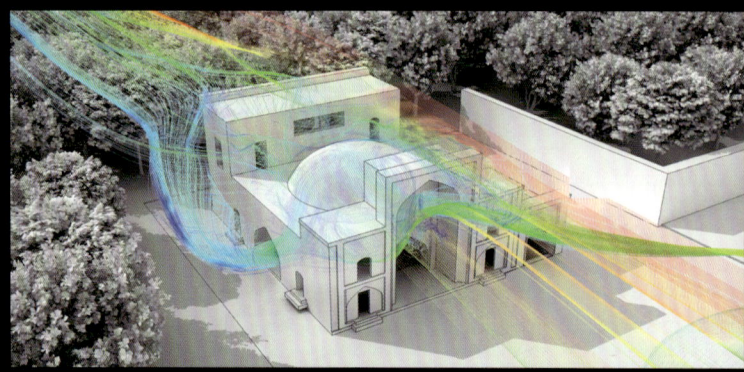

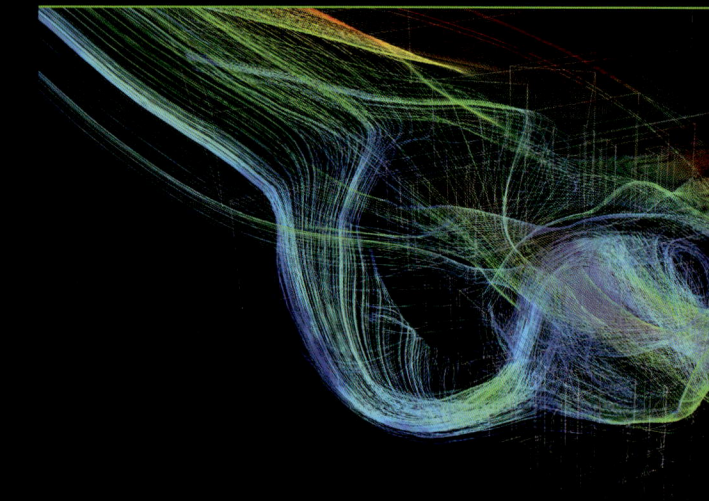

Sustainable Environment Association – SEA (Salmaan Craig, Mehran Gharleghi, Michael Hensel, Amin Sadeghy and Defne Sunguroğlu Hensel), Computational Fluid Dynamics Analysis, Sheikh Ahmad Jam Water Reservoir, Kashan, 2011
above and pp 28–9: In this reservoir, built around 1630, natural cross-ventilation evaporates water at the surface that helps maintain the cool temperature of the water. (Temporary software licences sponsored by EnSight®.)

SEA, Heat Transfer Analysis, Sheikh Ahmad Jam Water Reservoir, Kashan, 2011
opposite top: Ground and water entail two types of thermal inertia. Due to the large thermal mass volume, the temperature within the water storage remains constant while the outdoor temperature fluctuates significantly. The analysis of a 24-hour cycle from 19 to 20 April was carried out by RadTherm®.

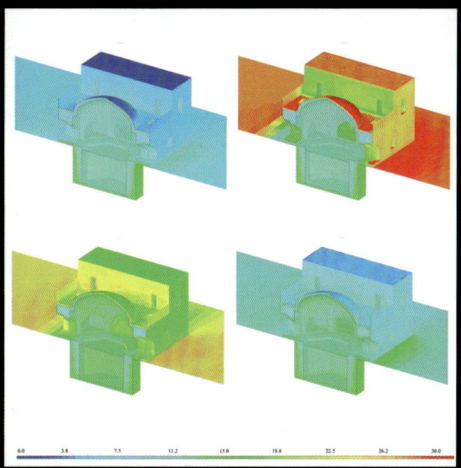

Water Cisterns

Subterranean Water Cisterns (*ab-anbar*) for the storage of drinking water were built either to collect water from qanats or, alternatively, where no qanats were available, to collect the water of sporadic torrential rainfall in the arid desert areas of the Iranian plateau. To enable proper cooling, resistance to water pressure and the impact of earthquakes, cisterns were built underground. Shahram Khora Sanizadeh of the Water Resource Institute in Iran estimates the storage capacity of historical water cisterns to vary from 300 to 3,000 cubic metres (10,594 to 105,944 cubic feet).[10] The cisterns were made from specially made bricks (*ajor ab anbari*) and mortar (*sarooj*), which consisted of 'sand, clay, egg whites, lime, goat hair, and ash in specific proportions, depending on location and climate'.[11] This type of mortar is thought to be quite resistant to water penetration. The cistern was enclosed by a vault or dome to maintain the water at a desired temperature and to protect it from dust and pollution. Access and maintenance was via stairs to the underground cistern that were typically covered by a vaulted entrance (*sardar*). The cisterns were filled during the winter with cold water at a temperature just above freezing. To keep the water cool throughout the year, the cisterns were in some regions equipped with multiple wind towers. The airflow across the water surface generated by the windcatchers removes evaporating water and prevents the warming up of the deeper layers of the water in the cistern as 'the heat from the air is almost entirely spent in evaporating the water at the surface'.[12]

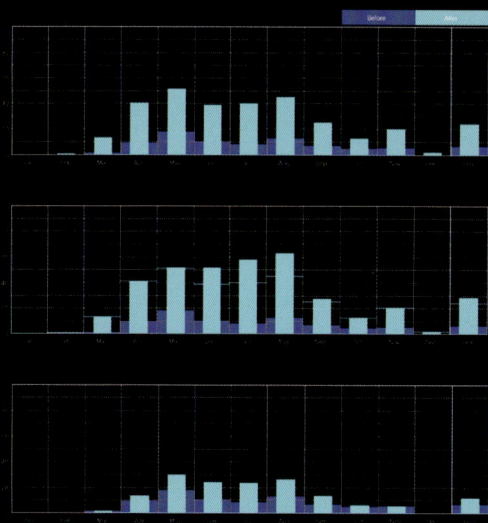

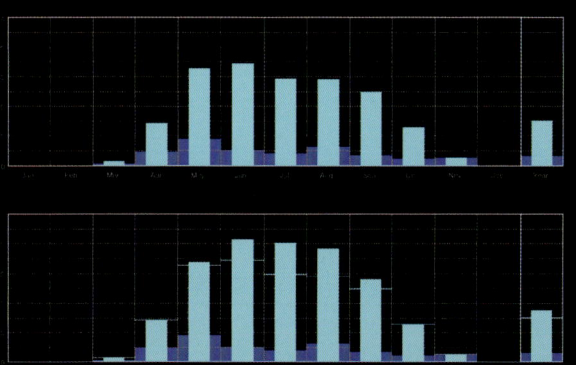

SEA, Passive Cooling Strategies, Kashan, Isfahan, 2011
above and left: The charts show the effectiveness of different passive cooling strategies in Kashan. From top to bottom: thermal mass effect, exposed mass and night purge ventilation, natural ventilation, direct evaporative cooling and indirect evaporative cooling.

Ice Houses

Some experts assume that ice houses originated in China around 800 BC.[13]

The purpose of the Iranian ice makers and ice houses (*yakh-chal*) was the production and storage of ice for human consumption. The ice houses commonly featured subterranean chambers covered by a large dome made from mud-brick that often reached 20 metres (66 feet) in height. Ice and snow could be brought from nearby mountains or harvested from frozen lakes in the winter, or produced next to the ice houses. It was then stored in the chamber and packed with straw or sawdust for insulation.

East–west-oriented shallow pools up to a length of 100 metres (328 feet) and more, and widths between 10 and 20 metres (33 and 66 feet) were backed on their southern side by a tall adobe wall that could shade the entire pool during the winter ice-making period, and protect the pools from the impact of the sun and wind-induced convective heat gain to reduce melting during the day. The accurate height of the east–west wall was of key importance: it needed to be high enough to shield the pool, but not so high that it would reduce the exposure of the water surface to the visible sky. The latter was essential to maintain maximum heat loss of the water through radiation. Additionally, each pool was flanked to the east and west by lower walls for the same purpose. During the cold winter nights the pools were filled with a shallow layer of water that would freeze overnight and could be harvested as ice in the morning.[14] The construction and management of the labour-intensive breaking, moving and storing of the ice required an integrative approach of immense accuracy. Various considerations needed to be correlated and calibrated: the critical dimensions of the structure, the labour associated with harvesting the ice, and the production of maximum quantities.

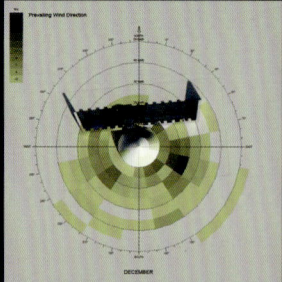
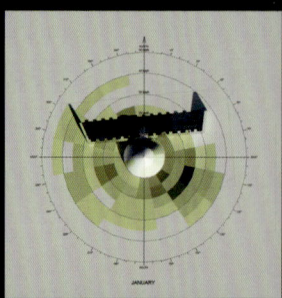
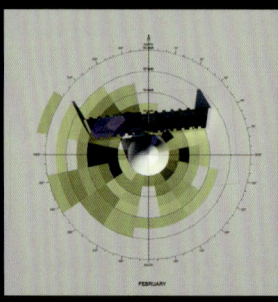

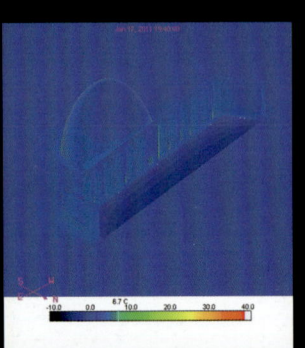
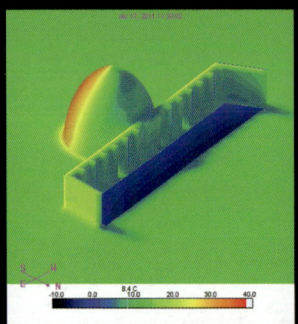

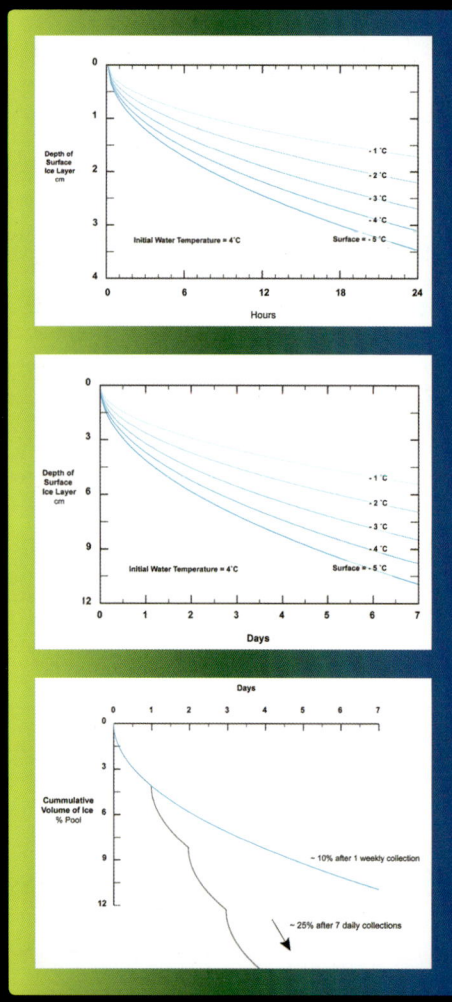

SEA, Heat Transfer Analysis, Ice House, Meybod, 2011
above: A transient thermal analysis of the ice house shows the evolution of temperatures over three days in winter. While the ambient temperature rarely dips below 0°C (32°F), the pond's exposure to the cold sky – coupled with the protection from the wind and sun afforded by the wall – create amenable conditions for the production of ice. Note that the surface of the water in the pond remains below zero, day and night.

SEA, Prevailing Wind Direction, Ice House, Meybod, 2011
top: The winter wind roses show that the pond is sheltered from the prevailing wind. At warmer than 0°C (32°F), the wind would reduce the rate of ice production or increase the rate of melting.

SEA, Ice Production Rate, Ice House, Meybod, 2011
above: Assuming conservatively that the body of water is an average 4°C (39.2°F), the rate of ice production over time – for progressively colder pond surface temperatures – can be calculated. These effects combine to give the curve that describes the rate of ice production its distinctive shape, as shown in the diagrams.

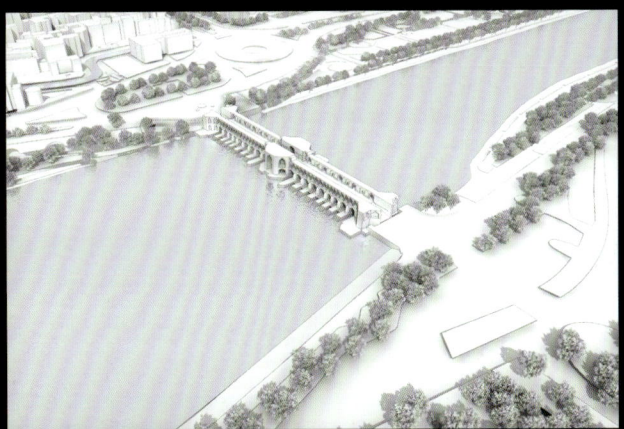

The Khaju Bridge

The Khaju Bridge (*pol-e khajoo*) was built around 1650 under the Safavid Shah Abbas II on the foundations of an older bridge spanning across the Zayandeh River in Isfahan. The 132-metre (433-foot) long and 14-metre (46-foot) wide two-storey masonry bridge has a 7.5-metre (25-foot) wide roadway on its upper storey that is framed on both sides by arched spaces, while the lower storey comprises a vaulted space that can only be reached by pedestrians. The bridge weir combines 18 low-flow deep channels equipped with sluice gates with stepped cascades for large flood flows, which serve to dissipate hydraulic energy.[15] The sluice gates regulate the water level of the Zayandeh River for the irrigation of upstream gardens and so on.

Its highly sophisticated hydraulic performance prompted Dr Mehrdad Hejazi at the Faculty of Engineering at the University of Isfahan to posit that the Khaju Bridge 'represents the ultimate achievement of Persian hydraulic engineering'.

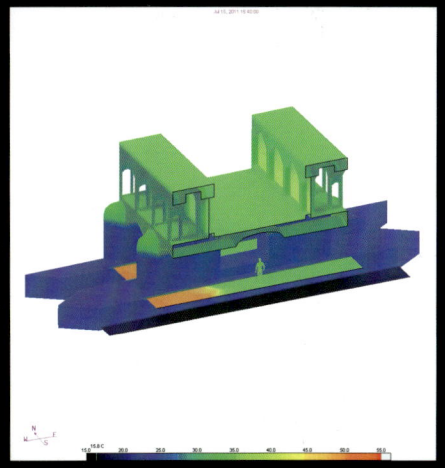

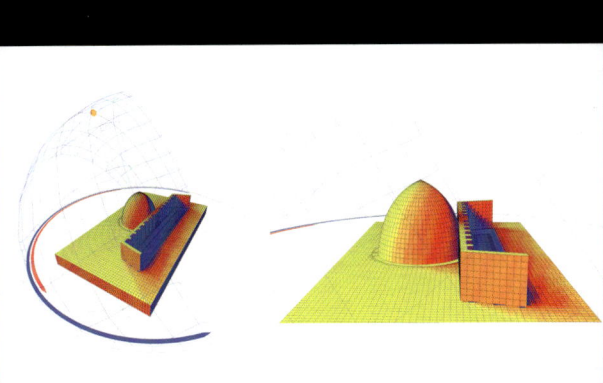

SEA, Solar Analysis, Ice House, Meybod, Yazd, 2011
bottom left: The wall was dimensioned to protect the water pond from the deleterious effects of sun and wind, without obstructing the pond's exposure to the clear night sky. This balance was essential in order to create ice in ambient temperatures above 0°C (32°F). The analysis shows that during the winter the pond receives no direct sunlight.

SEA, Axonometric and Section, Khaju Bridge (*pol-e khajoo*), Isfahan, 2011
top and centre left: The upper level of the Khaju Bridge (c 1650) serves as a roadway, while the lower comprises a vaulted public space.

SEA, Heat Transfer Analysis, Khaju Bridge (*pol-e khajoo*), Isfahan, 2011
centre and bottom right: The analysis shows the likely surface temperatures of the Khaju Bridge during an average summer afternoon. The combination of shading and high thermal mass along with the accelerated ventilation and evaporative cooling make the communal areas a comfortable environment.

Its highly sophisticated hydraulic performance prompted Dr Mehrdad Hejazi at the Faculty of Engineering at the University of Isfahan to posit that the Khaju Bridge 'represents the ultimate achievement of Persian hydraulic engineering'.[16] Yet its sophisticated fulfilment of its primary functions, its auxiliary relation to the urban circulation system and its central role in water management, are only part of the story. The need to construct a bridge with functional requirements related to water management was tackled in an opportunistic manner. The stepped chutes on its downstream side double up as seating for public use. Here, as well as in the tier of arches and vaulted space of the lower storey, evaporative cooling and the generated turbulent airflow generate a comfortable microclimate. From this perspective the spatial and material organisation of the bridge weir is inherently multifunctional. It thus combines a civic project with an unexpected provision of a climatically comfortable public space for appropriation and social assembly. Additional features are the pavilions for the shah placed on the upper level in the centre of the bridge facing up- and downstream.

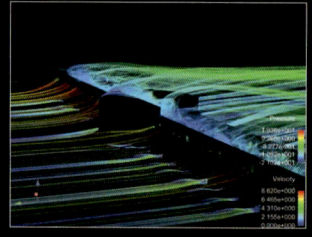

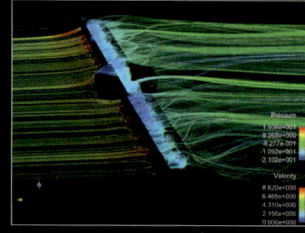

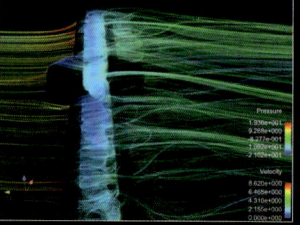

The bridge weir combines 18 low-flow deep channels equipped with sluice gates with stepped cascades for large flood flows, which serve to dissipate hydraulic energy. The sluice gates regulate the water level of the Zayandeh River for the irrigation of upstream gardens and so on.

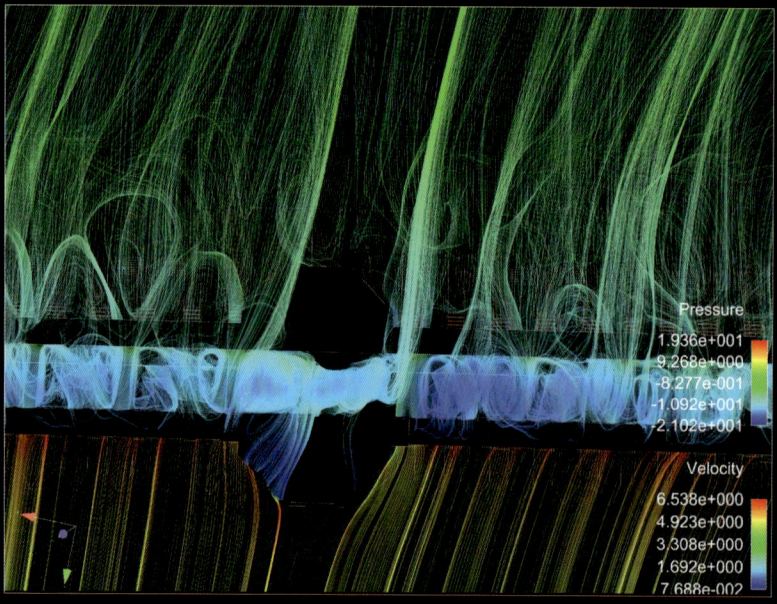

SEA, Computational Fluid Dynamic Analysis, Khaju Bridge (*pol-e khajoo*), Isfahan, 2011
The analysis suggests that the evenly spaced arched openings on the upper level allow wind to penetrate into the roadway at a lower speed, around 3.2 kilometres (2 miles) per second, creating a comfortable environment along the path.

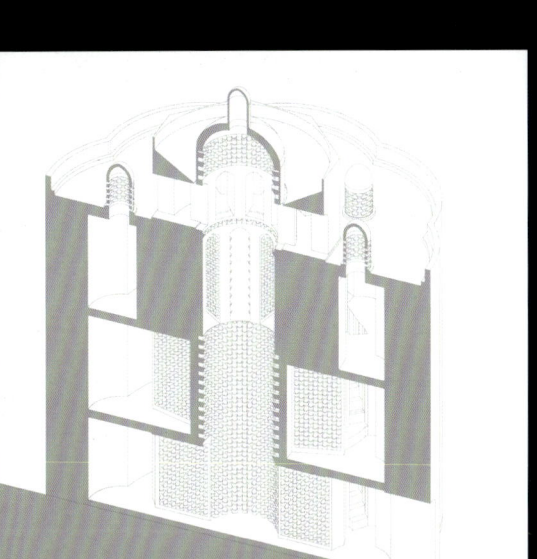
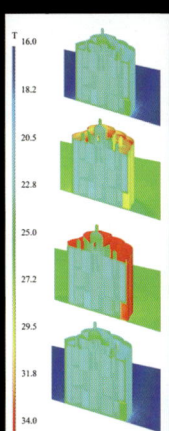

Pigeon Towers

During the Safavid period, another remarkable special-purpose building type flourished in the Isfahan region – the pigeon towers. The main function of these up to 20-metre (66-foot) tall buildings was to provide shelter for wild pigeons and to collect their dung as fertiliser for agriculture, in particular for growing melons, as well as for the softening of leather. Aryan Amirkhani and colleagues described that 'the pigeon towers of Isfahan are a perfect example of humans and nature working together in the name of mutual interest ... by attracting wild pigeons with seed and safe place to roost, the towers acted as a natural collection point for waste which could then be used as fertilizer'.[17] Circular or rectangular in plan with internally buttressed walls, pigeon towers could either be freestanding as single structures, or be integrated into the outer walls of gardens. The larger towers could house well over 10,000 pigeons. Such towers consisted either of a single hollow space or drum, or of an inner one enclosed by an outer drum. Some were organised in plan as eight connected drums around a central one, thus increasing the surface area of the interior and therefore also the number of pigeonholes. Atop the towers, turrets with honeycomb brickwork provided entry and exit for the pigeons. Humans accessed the towers usually only once a year to harvest the dung.[18]

Interestingly, structures for the exact same use can be found in Anatolia, whether the large rectangular dovecotes (*boranhane*) in the Diyarbakir region[19] or the often densely clustered half-above- and half-below-ground examples built on the steep slopes of the Kayseri region. The latter are characterised by a stone-made above-ground tower-like part (*burc*) that is rectangular, square, circular or ellipsoidal in plan and provides access for the pigeons, and a cave-like rock-hewn underground part (*kushane*) that accommodates the nests. A short tunnel and a door from the lower part of the slope provided human access for dung harvesting.[20]

Given the rich variation in articulation and use of these types of buildings it would be very interesting to undertake a comparative analysis and to see what can be learned from these examples for present structures that can house other species for the benefit of the human environment.

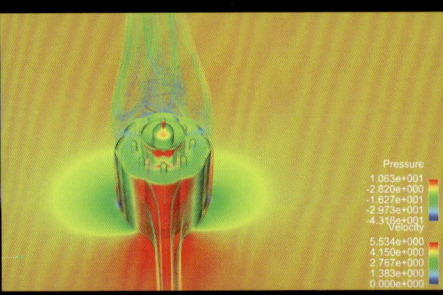
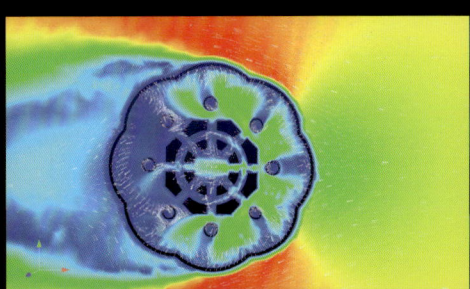

SEA, Axonometric Views and Heat Transfer Analysis, Pigeon Tower, Isfahan, 2011
top: The combination of thermal mass and openings in the turrets of pigeon towers maintained low internal surface temperatures and high ventilation rates. As this transient thermal analysis in RadTherm shows, the thickness of the multiple adobe walls is tuned to buffer daily temperature fluctuations effectively. (Sponsored by RadTherm®)

SEA, Computational Fluid Dynamic Analysis, Pigeon Tower, Isfahan, 2011
centre and bottom: The analysis of the Safavid period (1501–1736) pigeon tower shows how wind-driven ventilation occurs throughout the structure. In the absence of wind, the internal structure of the tower, and the difference in temperatures between top and bottom, would likely induce a natural stack effect. (Temporary licences sponsored by EnSight®)

Boroujerdi's House

During the 19th century, the illustrious architect Ostad Ali Maryam Kashani designed, among other projects, a number of highly sophisticated houses for wealthy clients in the city of Kashan. These include, most notably, the Tabatabaeis' House (Khaneh Tabatabaei-ha) (*c* 1850) and the Boroujerdi's House (Khane-ye Borujerdiha) (1857).

Surrounded by a densely built fabric, the Boroujerdi's House is introverted and dominated by a rectangular courtyard with its long axis stretching roughly from north-northeast to south-southwest. The plan organisation shows a sequence of linked spaces that constitute the entrance to the building from the north and lead into the courtyard. The latter is flanked by a series of linked narrow spaces and terminated by the main building mass to the south, which is organised as a matrix of interconnected spaces. This kind of organisation facilitates the correlation between climatic modulation, in this case passive ventilation and cooling, and the use of space. A pool in the courtyard facilitates heat loss through evaporation, and the plantation provides increased humidity and shading for the courtyard and building surfaces to prevent thermal gain. The arched and domed roofscape provides self-shading and thus the reduction of thermal impact. Intriguingly, the undulating earth-coloured roofscape resonates with that of Antoni Gaudí's Casa Milà in Barcelona (1910), not unlike other roofscapes in Kashan. Yet the highly expressive and sculptural roofscape of the Boroujerdi's House is clearly intended to be experienced as an artistic work in its own right. The house features three *badgir*-type chimney-like wind towers and a very sophisticated *khishkhan*-type dome. The former serves the entrance area in the north and the main living area to the south; its effect is further enhanced by the openings in the khishkhan-type central dome of the main hall. Interestingly, the placement of the openings and the internal geometric articulation and adornment of the dome are intricately related, and coordinate geometry with indirect light sources, thus demonstrating a highly coherent design down to the detail. In some areas, ventilated interstitial spaces are used between the outer roof surface and the inner ceilings, further preventing thermal gain.

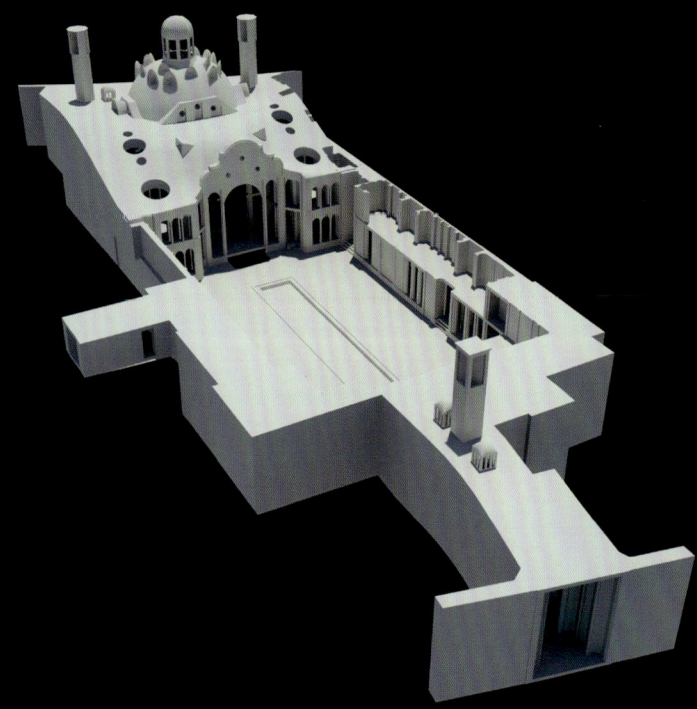

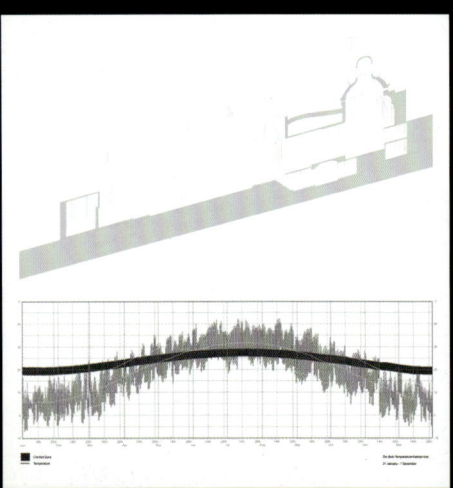

SEA, Dry Bulb Temperature, Boroujerdi's House (Khane-ye Borujerdiha), Kashan, 2011
left: The annual dry bulb temperature reveals dramatic temperature fluctuations through the different seasons. Passive climate strategies employed in the design of the Boroujerdi's House (1857) include a central courtyard, natural cross-ventilation, evaporative cooling, indirect light penetration, night purge ventilation and various types of wind towers.

SEA, 3-D model, Boroujerdi's House (Khane-ye Borujerdiha), Kashan, 2011
The images show the intricate relationship between the interior and the exterior of the dome. The design of the Boroujerdi's House demonstrates high-level integration of spatial quality and structural and environmental performance.

Looking Backwards to Project Forwards

The general performative capacities of the projects discussed above have been known and elaborated in expert papers over decades. Such capacities have here been situated as part of a new approach to the study of architectural history that focuses on architectural performance and is based on the notion of auxiliarity, as well as to employ contemporary environmental expertise and associated computer-aided analysis to examine the specific ranges of environmental modulation and functional integration in such projects. For projects with a narrow scope of function and exclusive of habitation by humans or other species, these ranges can be more constrained, while projects for human habitation provide for a more heterogeneous environment that offers choice. Further analysis will be necessary to unlock this complexity to inform contemporary designs, and to better understand the finely nuanced corresponding ranges to inform contemporary architecture and the sustainable provisions it will need to make. Described here are the beginnings of an effort that requires a broadly based interdisciplinary, forensic and projective take. ᴆ

Notes
1. Sheikh Muslih-uddin Sa'di Shirazi, *Prologue to the Gulistan (or Rose Garden)*, 1258, translated by Dr Iraj Bashiri, 2004. See: www.angelfire.com/rnb/bashiri/Sadi/SadiGulistan.pdf (accessed 12 September 2011).
2. JM Songel, *A Conversation With Frei Otto*, Princeton Architectural Press (New York), 2008, p 11.
3. D Leatherbarrow, 'Architecture Oriented Otherwise', Lecture at the Oslo School of Architecture and Design, 28 April 2011.
4. P Reitan, 'Sustainability Science – And What's Needed Beyond Science', *Sustainability: Science, Practice, & Policy* 1(1), 2005, pp 77–80. Online at: http://sspp.proquest.com/archives/vol1iss1/communityessay.reitan.pdf (accessed 12 September 2011).
5. See, for instance, E Loosley, *Messiah and Mahdi: Caucasian Christians and the Construction of Safavid Isfahan*, East & West Publishers (London), 2009, p 4. This defies the notion that so-called 'multiculturalism' is a contemporary condition that can be declared a 'failed project' by our politicians.
6. For a detailed elaboration of different types of windcatchers, their cross-sectional articulation and associated CFD analysis, see MM Zarandi, 'Analysis on Iranian Wind Catcher and its Effect on Natural Ventilation as a Solution Towards Sustainable Architecture (Case Study: Yazd)', *World Academy of Science, Engineering and Technology* 54, 2009, pp 574–579. Online at: www.waset.org/journals/waset/v54/v54-101.pdf (accessed 12 September 2011).
7. MN Bahadori, 'Passive Cooling Systems in Iranian Architecture', *Scientific American* 238(2), 1978, pp 144–54.
8. Ibid.
9. K Pirnia, 'Windtower', in G Memarian (ed), *Iranian Architecture*, Nashr Soroush Danesh (Tehran), 2008, pp 538–54.
10. SK Sanizadeh, 'Novel Hydraulic Structures and Water Management in Iran: A Historical Perspective', in M El Moujabber, M Shatanawi, G Trisorio Liuzzi, M Ouessar, P Laureano and R Rodriguez (eds), *Water Culture and Water Conflict in the Mediterranean Area*, CIHEAM-IAMB (Bari), 2008, pp 25–43. Online at: http://ressources.ciheam.org/om/pdf/a83/00800922.pdf (accessed 10 September 2011).
11. Ibid.
12. K Pirnia, op cit.
13. A Aryan and O Hanie, 'Historical Traditional Building Techniques in Some Iranian Vernacular Constructions', *The Heritage Journal*, Vol 4, 2009, pp 47–73.
14. K Pirnia, op cit.
15. H Chanson, 'Historical Development of Stepped Cascades for the Dissipation of Hydraulic Energy', *Transactions of the Newcomen Society for the Study of the History of Engineering and Technology* 71(2), 2001–2, pp 295–318.
16. MM Hejazi, *Historical Buildings of Iran: Their Architecture and Structure*, WIT Press (Southampton), 1997, pp 94–5.
17. A Amirkhani, P Baghaie, AA Taghvaee, MR Pourjafar and M Ansari, 'Isfahan's Dovecotes: Remarkable Edifices of Iranian Vernacular Architecture', *Middle East Technical University – Journal of the Faculty of Architecture* 26(1), 2009, pp 177–86. Online at: http://jfa.arch.metu.edu.tr/archive/0258-5316/2009/cilt26/sayi_1/177-186.pdf (accessed 12 September 2011).
18. Ibid.
19. A Bekleyen, 'The Dovecotes of Diyarbakir: The Surviving Example of a Fading Tradition', *The Journal of Architecture* 14(4), 2009, pp 451–64.
20. V Imamo lu, M Korumaz and C Imamo lu, 'A Fantasy in Central Anatolian Heritage: Dove Cotes and Towers in Kayseri', *Middle East Technical University – Journal of the Faculty of Architecture* 22(02), 2005, pp 79–90. Online at: http://jfa.arch.metu.edu.tr/archive/0258-5316/2005/cilt22/sayi_2/79-90.pdf (accessed 12 September 2011).

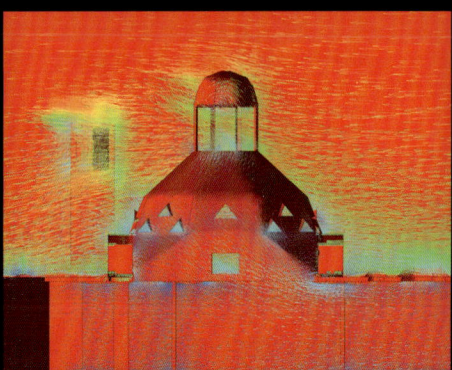

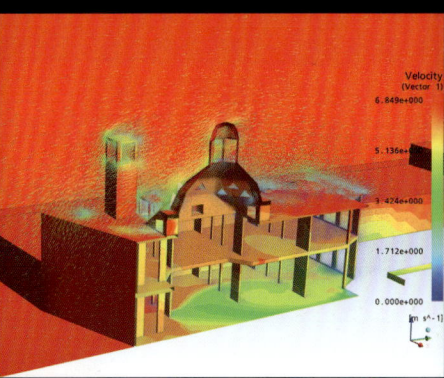

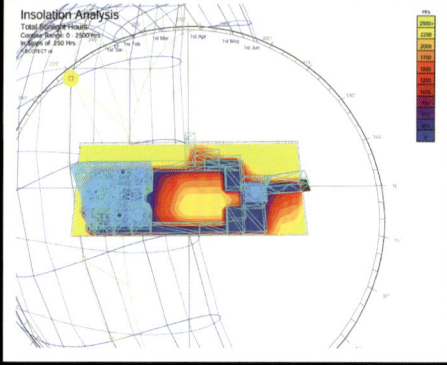

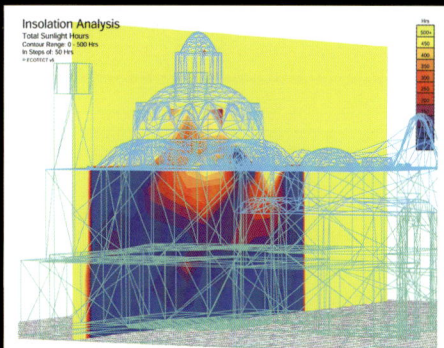

SEA, Computational Fluid Dynamic Analysis, Boroujerdi's House (*Khane-ye Borujerdiha*), Kashan, 2009
The central dome of the Boroujerdi's House provides highly sophisticated ventilation. Spilling water on the plants at the top part of the dome around noon helped to cool down the air while other roof openings allowed for further air and indirect light penetration.

SEA, Solar Analysis, Boroujerdi's House (*Khane-ye Borujerdiha*), Kashan, 2009
The analysis shows that the annual direct sunlight exposure is considerably lower on the south side, which is the reason why it was intensively used during the summer. The bottom image reveals that the annual direct sunlight penetration via the dome into the lower levels of the living area is almost zero. The combination of indirect sunlight penetration and natural ventilation maximises the passive cooling performance of the house.

Text © 2012 John Wiley & Sons Ltd. Images: pp 26–7, 30–6, 37(r) © SEA – Sustainable Environment Association: Salmaan Craig, Mehran Gharleghi, Michael Hensel, Amin Sadeghy, and Defne Sunguroğlu Hensel; p 37(l) © SEA – Sustainable Environment Association: Mehran Gharleghi and Amin Sadeghy

PERSIAN GARDENS

Nasrine Faghih and Amin Sadeghy

AND
LANDSCAPES

The verdant gardens of ancient Persia are a testament to this highly developed culture's resourcefulness and ability to not only source and direct water and irrigate the land in a hostile environment, but then to transform it into a manmade paradise. Here, **Nasrine Faghih and Amin Sadeghy** provide a historic outline of Persian garden typologies and their evolution over time, focusing on the central kiosk within the enclosed garden and highlighting the synergy between climate, resources and place.

THE PARADIGM OF A SHARED UTOPIA

The Persian garden has been since the beginning of time a borrowed landscape, a world of perfect harmony where the climate is moderate, the flora is abundant and a smooth light always glimmers. According to legend, Zoroaster made a journey to a heavenly landscape where he crossed a four-branch river and received the eternal light. While Persian gardens exuded the ideals of a heavenly landscape, they were also the expression of strict environmental performance. The provision and distribution of water in arid lands and the urge to create more docile habitable microclimates led Iranians to develop the acumen for organising colossal operations to find and direct water hidden deep under mountains. The resulting garden kiosks they designed achieved great climatic performance in an adverse landscape. They were privileged, comfortable places where architecture overcame a hostile environment. While this article reviews the historic outline of Persian garden typologies and their evolution in time and place, it also for the first time applies analytic tools to this type of project. The investigation focuses on the central kiosk within its enclosed garden, in order to understand the synergy between climate, resources and place, revealing the genius of traditional master architects and how they utilised natural elements to create an architecture that both controlled and moderated the climate.

Celebrations in Honour of the Birth of Humayun in the Chahar Bagh of Kabul, Mogul miniature, 1508

The first Persian garden on record is Pasargadae,[1] built in approximately 600 BC by Achaemenid emperor Cyrus, which is based on the Zoroastrian division of the universe in four parts, four seasons or four elements: water, wind, soil and fire. The Persian conquerors of the mountainous arid Iranian plateau re-created this imaginary landscape in garden cities, called *paraedizo* ('enclosures', in ancient Persian). The city of Pasargadae, the most complete vestige of an Achaemenid garden city, covered an immense area and was divided into four distinct sections separated by two main watercourses. This regular ensemble of palaces and gardens built on fortified terraces became the prototype for the construction of garden cities throughout the Achaemenid empire. Vestiges of several other garden palaces of this type reveal the importance that Iranians accorded to building paradise gardens as a founding act.[2] The tradition of erecting monumental garden cities on a quadripartite matrix continued on a large scale throughout the pre-Islamic period (224–651) in Sassanid settlements such as Bishapur, Gur and Siraf.

It is in these verdant gardens of ancient Persia that we discover their symbolic sources and aesthetic ideals that endured and developed as the model for major royal settlements in newly conquered lands on the Iranian plateau, as well as in Syria and

Andalusia, throughout the early Islamic periods. This tradition then spread into central Asia and Mogul architecture, finding its highest expression in the 16th century with the gardens of the Safavids (1501–1736).

A SHORT HISTORY OF AN *IMAGO MUNDI*
Madinat-al-Zahra, Cordoba, Andalusia, Spain

Masterplanning a city on a four-part garden, or *chahar bagh*, matrix as in the classical age first occurred with the advent of Islam in Andalusia, southern Spain. And in 936, the Abd al-Rahman III (912–61), Caliph of Cordoba, undertook the construction of an immense garden city modelled on the Sassanid (224–651) paradise gardens. Madinat-al-Zahra, built on the slopes of the Sierra Morena mountains, towering over Cordoba, strongly echoed the garden cities of the Sassanid. Erected on an elevated platform, the city is divided into four sections by two main alleys. A reception hall sits at the crossing of the two alleys and overlooks water basins in each of the four sides. The upper sections are destined for royal residences and ceremonial halls whereas the lower sections shelter houses and other utilitarian buildings. The intention of creating a landscape made of lines of vegetation interrupted by transparent edifices (miradors) open to bodies of water announces a new architecture.

Samarkand, Uzbekistan

Some four centuries later, Timur (1370–1405), the founder of the Timurid dynasty that extended from Persia to Northern India, found a favourable climate to build a garden city at Samarkand, now in contemporary Uzbekistan. He followed the tradition of Persian royal cities, creating a series of gardens. Water was abundant here and the variety of trees provided the cool shade that poets and guests admired and eulogised over.[3] The gardens of Samarkand were the inspiration behind the Persian poetry and the Timurid miniatures that glorify the art of celebration in a landscape made of delicate edifices dotted among the trees and the flowers. They went to ruin in less than a century, however their legacy remained and has been an inspiration to garden designers to this day. Joining functional with imaginary, microcosm with macrocosm, the archetype of the Persian garden has been chosen in arid zones where water had to be collected and distributed with parsimony in order to create gardens.[4]

The Persian garden has been since the beginning of time a borrowed landscape, a world of perfect harmony where the climate is moderate, the flora is abundant and a smooth light always glimmers.

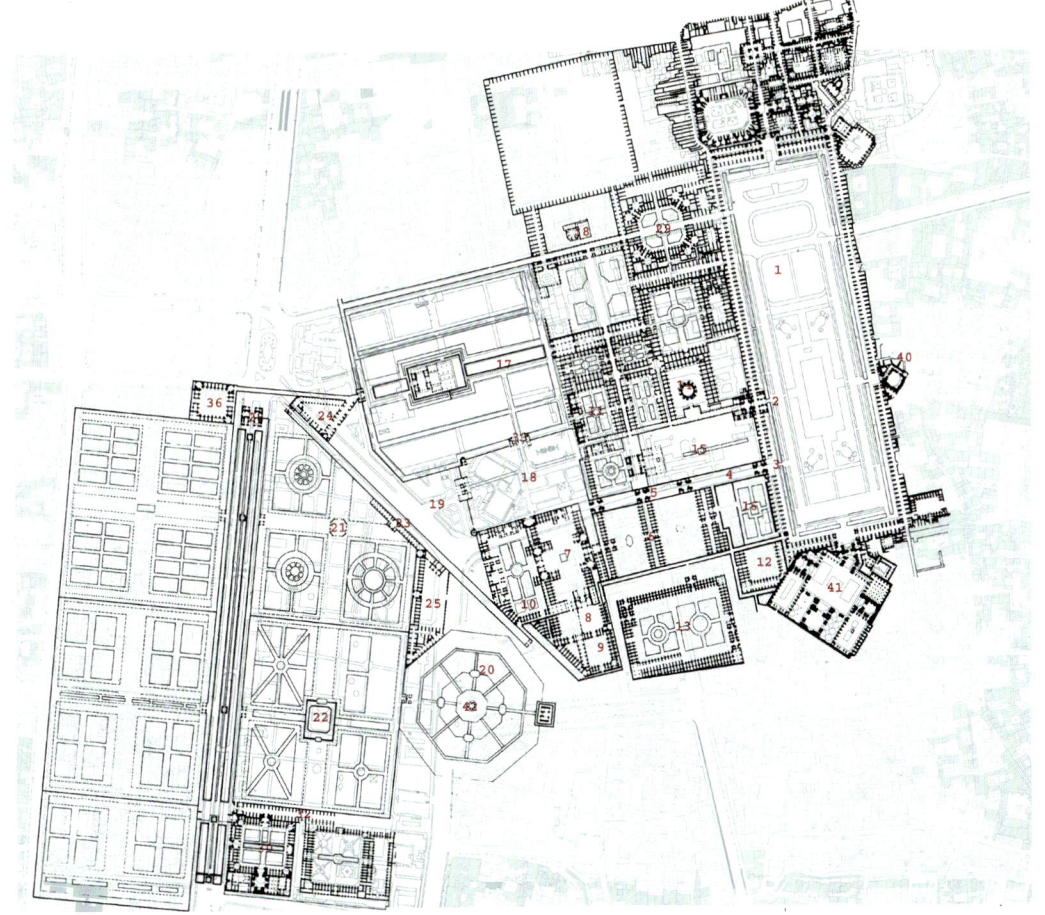

Sheikh Bahai, Naqsh-e Jahan Square and Chahrbagh Street, Isfahan, Iran, 17th century
The site plan of Naqsh-e Jahan Square: (1) Shah Square; (2) Ali Qapu Palace; (3) gate palace; (4) second entrance gate to the residential district; (5) third and fourth gates to the residential district; (6) dwelling of the blind princes; (7) royal house; (8) promenades and houses; (9) residential areas and basements; (10) Queen Mother's house; (11) storage and warehouses; (12) royal kitchens; (13) jewellery maker's workshops; (14) post office; (15) stables; (16) horse grooms' court; (17) garden of Chehel Sotun; (18) private garden; (19) vineyard; (20) rose garden; (21) Kaargah garden; (22) Hasht Behesht garden; (23) road to the city gate; (24) royal stable; (25) staff stables and dwellings; (26) water master's houses; (27) water pump room; (28) Jahan Nama Palace; (29) royal caravanserai; (30) Queen Mother's madrasa; (31) caravanserai of Shah's mother; (32) bazaar; (33) orangery; (34) Takht garden; (35) garden; (36) caravanserai; (37) offices; (38) Khosro Agha bathhouse; (39) Main bazaar gate; (40) Sheikh Lotf-o Allah Mosque; (41) Shah Mosque; (42) Goldaste Pavilion.

Isfahan, Iran

Two hundred years after the establishment of Samarkand, Shah Abbas I (Shah Abbas the Great) (1571–1629) of Persia laid down the foundation for the imperial city of Isfahan. He was charmed by the mild climate of the Isfahan plain, situated at the centre of the Iranian plateau, and undertook the planning of the city assisted by scholars and philosophers, such as the legendary Sheikh Bahai (1547–1621). The rate of flow of the Zayandeh River and its seasonal variations were calculated, so that the city's area was determined by the water's reach and pressure. The size of each parcel of land was determined in meetings between lawyers, master architects, garden designers and botanists. The final project is a city set on a series of gardens that is open to the natural landscape. On a longitudinal axis, Chahar Bagh Avenue symbolically links the country's north to the south, and the imperial city joins the medieval town via a geometrical detour, carefully oriented according to the summer solstice. As a result, the city's Naqsh-e Jahan Square is on a perfect north–south axis; at its northern end is the monumental portico of the Grand Bazaar, the Qaysariah, with the future Shah Mosque at its southern end. Two bridges overhang the Zayandeh River and extend the city plan to the agricultural land it irrigates. Jean Chardin, a French traveller who visited Isfahan in 1671, reported:

> The long boulevard called Isfahan Course is definitely a novelty. This is to my knowledge the most beautiful alley. Spacious promenades are shadowed by several ranks of plane trees; the boulevard is flanked at both sides by a suite of gardens linked to each other by pools and watercourses in cascade.[5]

Isfahan is probably the first post-medieval example of an open city, with no fortifications, deliberately oriented towards the landscape. The river, spanned by two magnificent bridges launching the city's view towards the surrounding territory, even today triggers a strong sensation.

As Chardin describes them, the green squares planted with all sorts of flowers evoke the blossoming fields of the 14th-century Alhambra Palace in Granada, Andalusia, and the verdant city of Samarkand in Uzbekistan.

Before Isfahan, palace gardens included residences, commerce, public buildings, orchards and vegetable prairies, but they were always enclosed. In 15th-century Herat, in present-day Afghanistan and the capital city of the Timurid descendants, and later Kazvin, the capital of Tahmasb I (1514–76), founder of the Safavid dynasty, were both cities set in gardens. In Kazvin, the government palace (*dowlatkhaneh*), the ladies' palace (*khalvatkhaneh*) and the aristocratic residences were laid on a *chahar bagh* matrix and connected to each other through planted alleys and watercourses punctuated by square pools in the centre or at the four corners. These urban complexes were always surrounded by walls.[6]

Isfahan is probably the first post-medieval example of an open city, with no fortifications, deliberately oriented towards the landscape. The river, spanned by two magnificent bridges launching the city's view towards the surrounding territory, even today triggers a strong sensation. Isfahan's plan announces the beginning of a new century with no fear of the exterior world and with no rejection of an unpredictable nature. Nature is controlled, irrigated, made fertile, and therefore becomes beautiful. It deserves to be contemplated. The archetype of the enclosed garden divided into four parts is deployed in a series of landscaped gardens where the principles of unity, repetition, sequence and equilibrium can be found.

The city's plan was designed in three phases. The grand square, the bazaar and its monumental portico were conceived in the first phase. Construction started in 1591 and lasted five

Sheikh Bahai, Chehel Sotun Palace (Palace of Forty Columns) and Naqsh-e Jahan Square, Isfahan, 17th century
Aerial view showing the relationship of the palace garden to Naqsh-e Jahan Square and Ali Qapu Palace.

Shazdeh Garden (Bagh-e Shazdeh), Mahan, Kerman Province, 1850–60
left: Aerial view of the garden. The qanat directs water from the mountains and dramatically changes the microclimate of the desert into a lush garden.

below: Exposure to the body of water in the garden decreases mean radiant temperature and increases humidity. Mist caused by the water fountain produces an evaporative cooling effect, decreases air temperature and leads to an increased comfort level.

below centre: Qanat constructed as a series of vertical wells, connected by gently sloping tunnels, efficiently directs water to the surface.

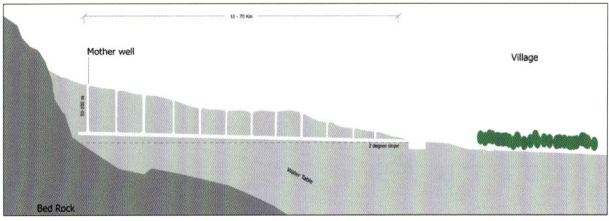

years. The second phase was launched in 1596 and centred on the creation of Chahar Bagh, the longitudinal avenue, a four-line park that runs between the northern gate and the monumental Bridge of 33 Arches (*si-o-se pol*). This project defined the area of future garden palaces, the appointment of land and the line of canals. It took another seven years for the king and his high-ranking officials to build their residences in between the sequence of Persian gardens and move to Isfahan. And, finally, in the early years of the 17th century, Isfahan became the official capital of Iran.[7]

The art of designing gardens was an intellectual game among Persian nobility, scholars and artists. The challenge consisted in taming vast arid territories and turning them into fertile agricultural land. In less than two decades an important area about one kilometre beyond the Khaju Bridge (*pol-e khajoo*) was developed into vast estates. The entrance gate (*dargah*) to each was designed with a central two-storey kiosk with balconies (*balakhaneh*) looking over the boulevard. The boulevard itself followed a *chahar bagh* scheme, cut by four watercourses serving to irrigate this sequence of farms.

The example of Isfahan is adopted in other places around Iran, with cities planned on a similar garden pattern. The garden city of Ashraf was another significant project undertaken by Shah Abbas. This complex, visited by the Italian traveller Pietro della Valle while under construction, is a terrace city built on slopes overlooking the Caspian Sea. It had several residences, a bazaar and other utilitarian buildings, and served as the royal summer residence up until the 19th century.[8]

The Isolated Desert Garden

But imperial garden cities are not the only example of paradise gardens in Iran. Throughout the Middle Ages, the *chahar bagh* tradition was perpetuated in large extramural agricultural estates. Archaeological data from which we can get a clear idea of the Iranian king's garden palaces contemporary with those of Andalusia are cruelly missing, but an abundant literature left by memorialists of this period helps to measure the relevance of gardens around medieval cities; formal gardens with palaces and geometrically set watercourses and planted walkways are regularly mentioned.

Another type of Persian garden can be found on the edge of cities, or in the middle of the desert. These walled enclaves are built at the precise point where the underground irrigation system emerges. The water is collected and channelled in the perfect archetypal *chahar bagh* design of these gardens. When the garden is built on a strong slope, terraces are provided and the watercourse runs in a sequence of cascades like in the Shazdeh Garden (Bagh-e Shazdeh), built between 1850 and 1860, in Mahan, Kerman province. Most commonly, the garden is traced on a slight slope and is crossed by a main boulevard in the middle of which runs a watercourse. The desert garden follows

43

These extraordinary artificial climates created in such a hostile environment have encouraged us to explore in depth the environmental behaviour of one in particular.

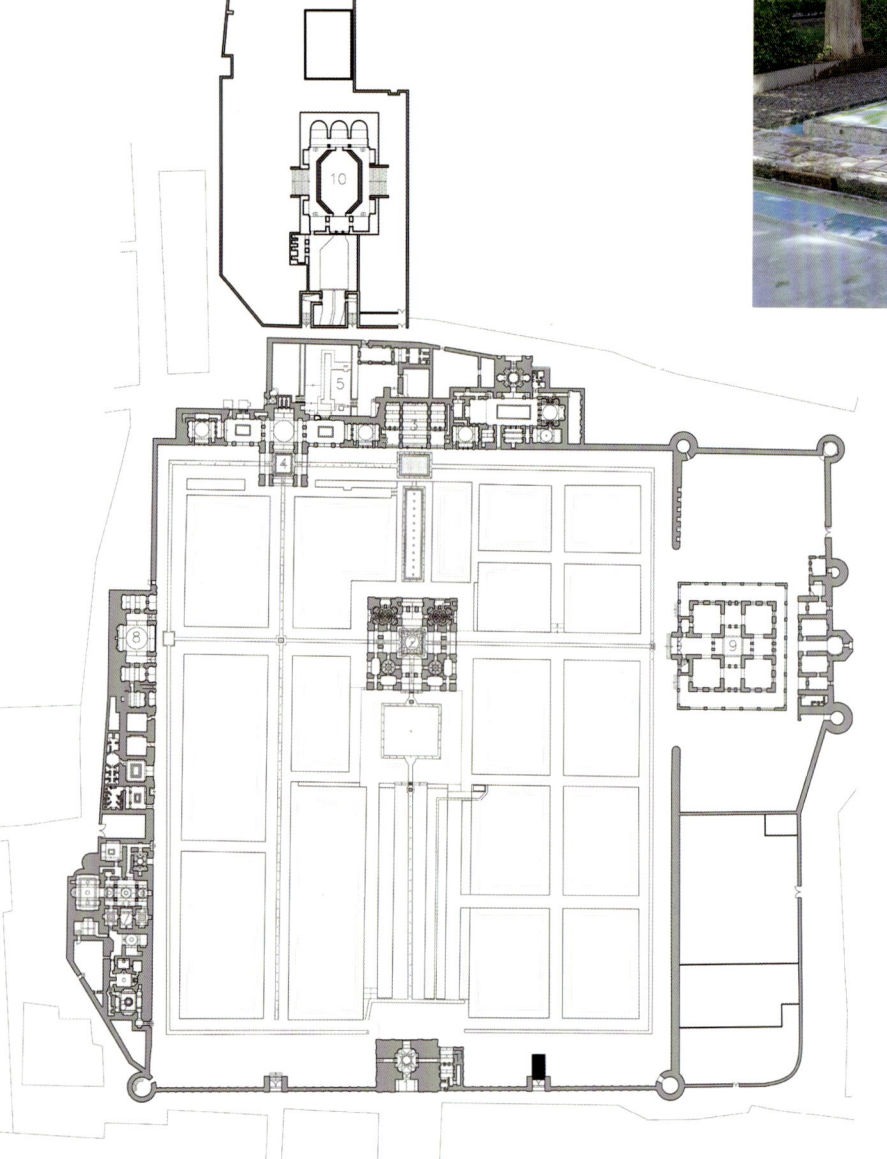

Fin Garden, Kashan, Isfahan, 1629
top: Aerial view showing the arrangement of trees, the gate building and central kiosk. The higher-elevation Soleymaniye spring can be seen at the top of the image.

centre: View from the reception palace towards the central kiosk showing water circulation. Fountains are connected to the kiosk's pool through an underground canal.

left: Fin Garden site plan: (1) Gate building; (2) central kiosk; (3) royal audience; (4) ladies' koushk (summer kiosk open from four sides); (5) ladies' water spring; (6) main walkway; (7) bathhouse; (8) private kiosk; (9) later constructed museum; (10) Soleymaniye spring, source of the qanat.

a strict geometry, and the size of each plot reflects the need to create shadow or to grow flowers.

The vision of these green paradises at the foot of bare mountains along the roads in Iran still has a magical effect today, and stepping into them, one is surprised by the cool atmosphere and the light breeze, while the sound of water and the singing of birds leads you into a world of dreams.

These extraordinary artificial climates created in such a hostile environment have encouraged us to explore in depth the environmental behaviour of one in particular. Fin Garden[9] is situated 6 kilometres (3.7 miles) west of Kashan on the outskirts of the abundant Soleymaniye spring. The garden, like most of those that have been created in the desert, has been there since ancient times. Travellers in the Middle Ages referred to Fin Village, with its greenery and cool climate, as a pleasant stop. The present garden is another project of Shah Abbas, who laid the stones of a formal walled garden in this naturally privileged location, halfway between his ancient capital, Kazvin, and the new one in Isfahan.

Fin is a large walled enclave (about a kilometre square) with four control towers. The garden scheme is a perfect

top: Interior view of the Fin Garden central kiosk illustrating the transparency, lightness and intricate design and detail of the Rasmibandi ornamentation on the soffit of the dome, the wooden pattern of the balustrade and the spring in central space.

bottom: Water is delivered by qanat springs from the centre of the kiosk and branches out in four directions into the garden, reducing the temperature by mist effect and radiation.

Travellers in the Middle Ages referred to Fin Village, with its greenery and cool climate, as a pleasant stop.

Sustainable Environment Association (SEA), Fin Garden Environmental Study, 2010–11
Total sunlight radiation analysis of the Fin Garden on 21 June.

top left: Annual sun-path diagram showing the sun trajectory over 12 months.

top right: North aerial view of the garden revealing that the kiosk is in shade for more than eight hours during the hottest summer day.

bottom: The west-facing facade demonstrates how the porous form of the kiosk building creates self-shading and reduces direct solar radiation. Its orientation creates two zones of summer and autumn comfort.

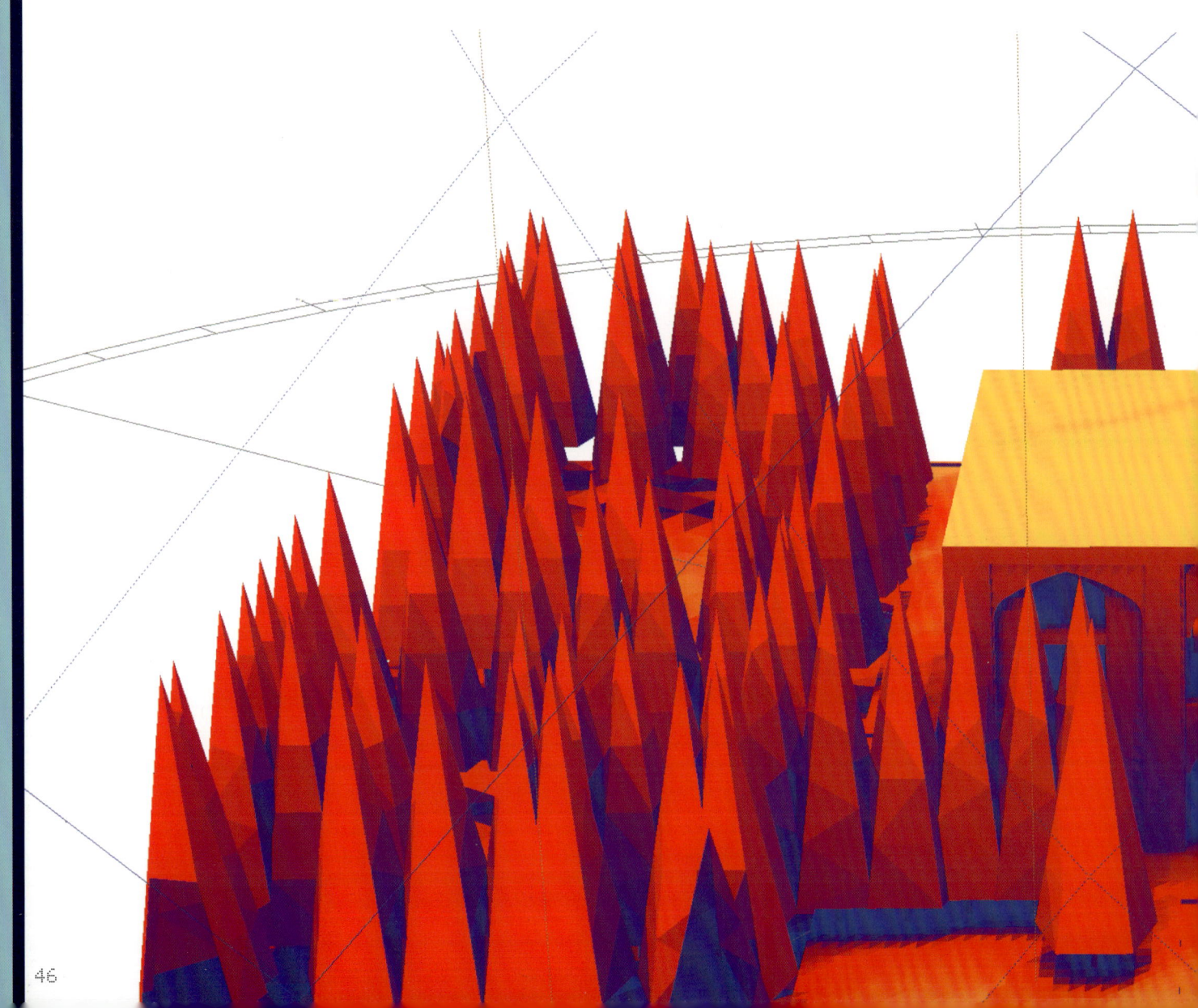

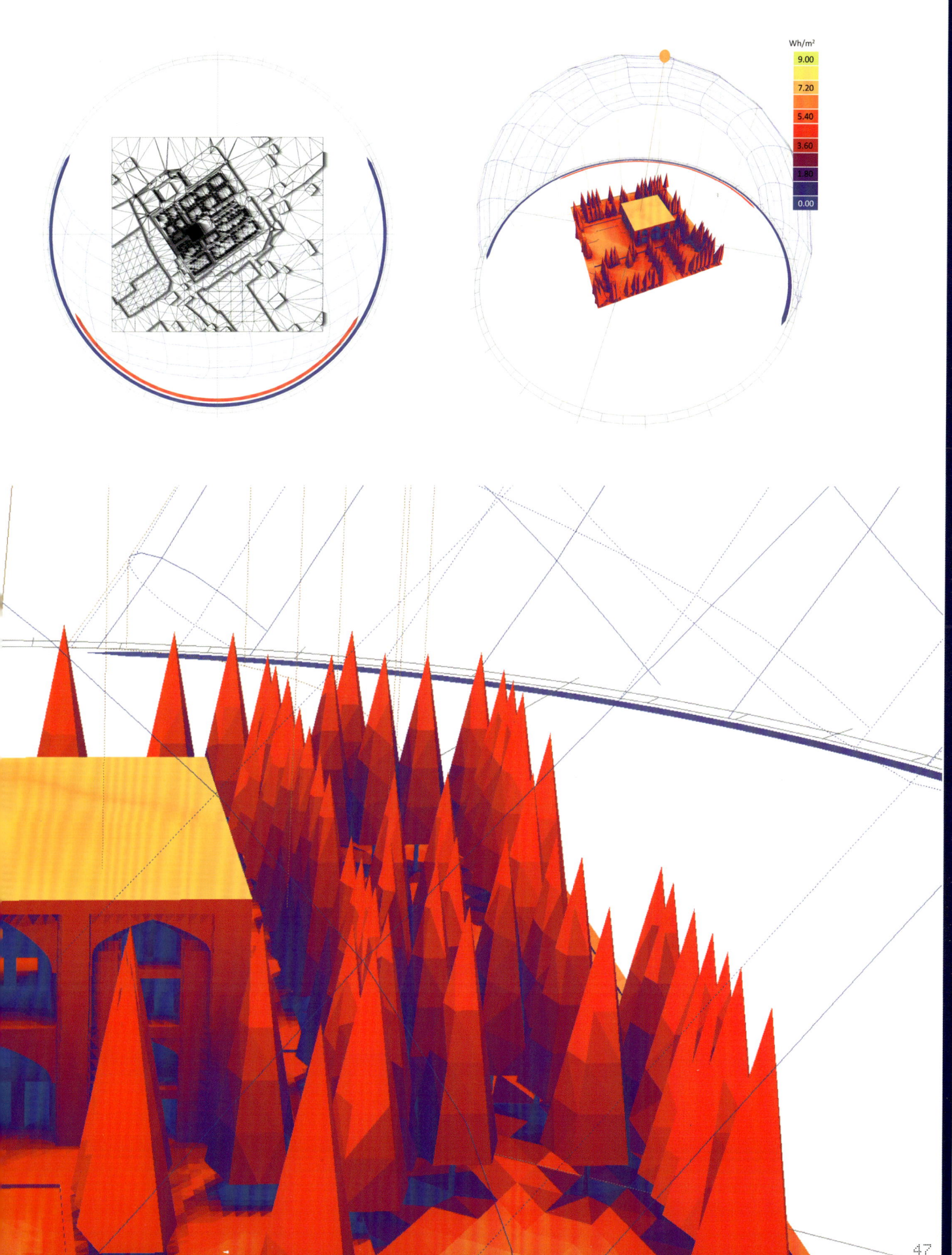

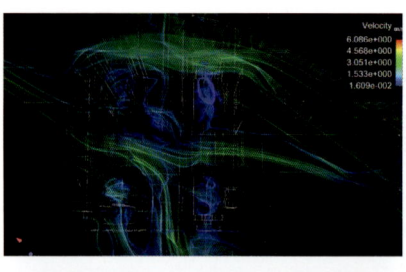

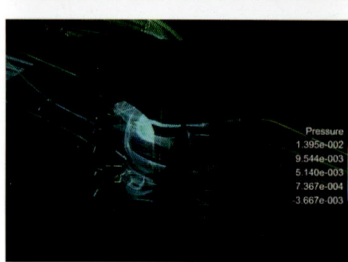

It is one of the most beautiful examples of the Persian garden with its majestic main alley crossed by streams and pools.

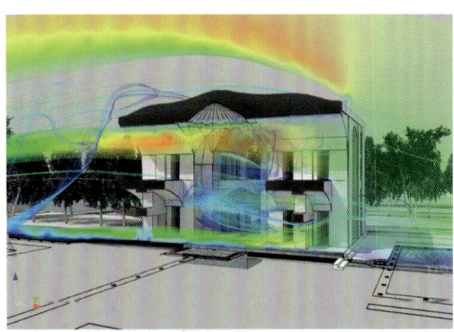

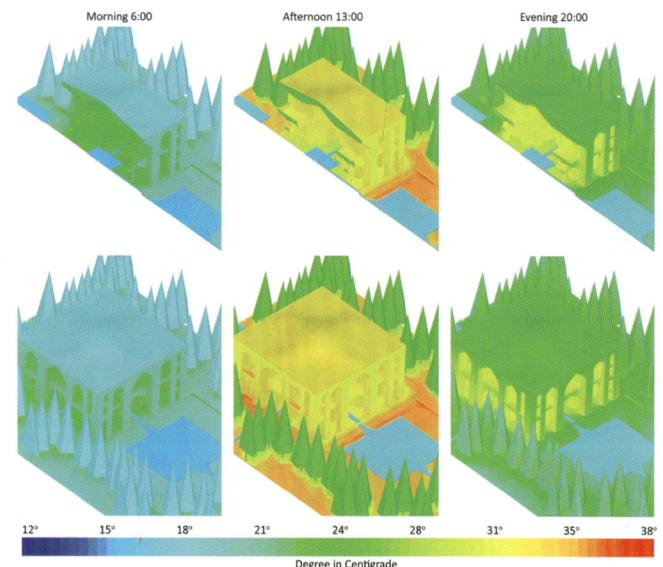

CFD analysis.
top: Section of the kiosk demonstrating wind direction and speed deceleration from the higher elevation on the first floor to the ground floor, which helps to ventilate warm air at the higher elevation and a comfortable wind speed at lower levels. The water table at the centre of the kiosk with fountains and natural ventilation enhances the evaporative cooling effect. Air movement above the water increases the humidity and evaporative cooling effect, leading to an improvement in the comfort level.

bottom: Perspective of the kiosk explaining wind direction and speed. Form and porosity in the kiosk help the building to work as a large wind-catching mechanism enhancing natural ventilation. The general orientation of the garden, 45° towards the southeast facilitates an increase of pressure difference on opposite sides of the building.

CFD analysis.
top: Flow of air over the landscape and within the kiosk demonstrating wind speed and direction. The porosity of the structure enhances the pressure differences and wind speed, which decreases as it enters the main space and continues to decrease as it branches into the rooms.

above: Transient thermal analysis of the Fin Garden: surface temperature. The diagram shows the beneficial effect of thermal mass. The roof surface heats to above 30°C (86°F) during the day and cools to near 15°C (59°F) at night. This is helped by the effect of night-sky radiative cooling, while the internal mass of the roof stays at a moderate 24°C (75°F) throughout the day leading to comfortable radiant temperatures inside the kiosk. The analysis was carried out on a 24-hour cycle from 19 to 20 April by RadTherm® (see article on pp 26–37).

chahar bagh crossed by two main walkways with a kiosk open to four views at the cross-section. It is one of the most beautiful examples of the Persian garden with its majestic main alley crossed by streams and pools. Fin Garden succeeds in combining a clear geometry of visible wide walkways with the intimacy of several shadowed enclosures. The original garden comprises a two-storey portal, the central kiosk, facing a pool. The elaborate waterways, with their small fountains, produce a murmur. A winter kiosk, a ladies' building and a bathhouse were added in the early 18th century. Later, in the 19th century, the addition of a residence and other buildings framed the verdant garden on its two lateral sides. The cool shade and the subtle play of water and kiosk mirroring each other are still today one of the precious secrets of Iranian architecture.

Chahar bagh and its major components – the kiosk, alleys, waterways, pools and planted parterres – far beyond a formal recall of the universe, translate a practical layout principle of water regulation, soil and plant treatment and building. In traditional Persian agricultural treatise, *chahar bagh* appears just like a simple manual for gardeners, as a good way of mapping out land in order to obtain an ideal garden. ∆

Notes
1. Pasargadae was designated a World Heritage site in February 2011, along with eight other gardens in Iran. See Mohammad Hassan Talebian, 'Persian Gardens World Heritage Document', UNESCO, 2011.
2. Nasrine Faghih, 'Bandar Siraf', *Honar va Mardom*, 1975, pp 159–60.
3. Roy Gonzalez de Clavijo, *Narrative of the Spanish Embassy to the Court of Timur at Samarkand in the Years 1403–1406*, trans Guy Le Strange [1928], Laurier Books (London), 2002.
4. Nasrine Faghih, 'Chahar Bagh, le paradigme du jardin Islamique', *Gardens of Iran*, Tehran Museum of Contemporary Art (Tehran), 2003.
5. Jean Chardin, *Voyages du chevalier Chardin en Perse et autres lieux de l'Orient: Nouvelle édition, conférée sur les trois éditions originales et augmentée par L Langlès*, Tome 8 (French edn), Adamant Media Corporation, 1723.
6. Maria Zuppe, *Palais et jardins, Le complexe royal des premiers safavids à Qazvin*, Res Orientalis VIII (Bures-sur-Yvette), 1996.
7. Mahvash Alemi, 'Chahar Bagh', *Journal of the Islamic Design Research Center*, 1986. And RD McChesney, *Four sources on the building of Isfahan*, Muqarnas V, 1988.
8. Ashraf is among the nine gardens on the World Heritage list in February 2011. See also Yves Porter, *Les jardins d'Ashraf vues par Henri Violet*, Res Orientalis VIII (Bures-sur-Yvette), 1996.
9. Fin Garden was the subject of an environmental survey by the Sustainable Environmental Association (SEA): Amin Sadeghy, Nasrine Faghih, Mehran Gharleghi, Salmaan Craig and Michael Hensel, during 2010/11.

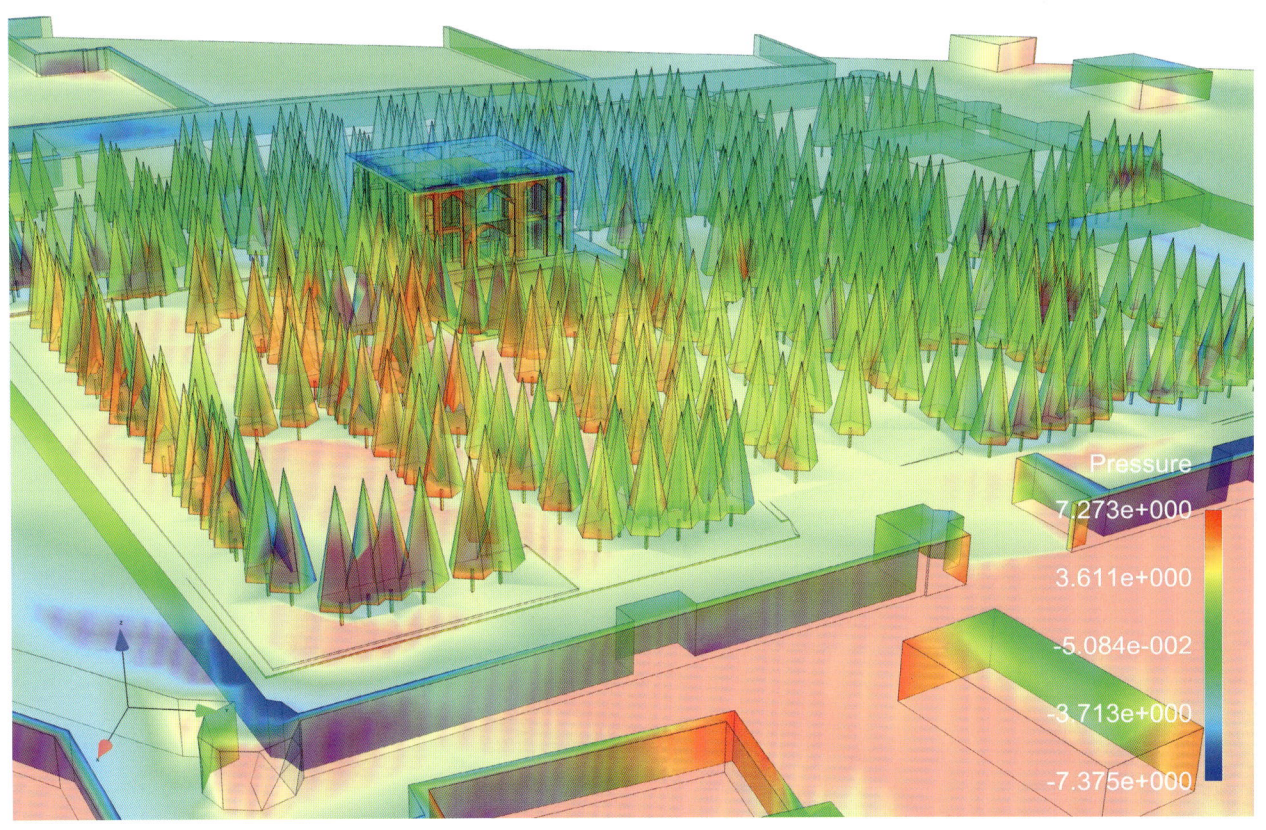

Diagram showing pressure difference throughout the Fin Garden site while wind blows west to east. This produces the high-pressure areas (red) in the west-facing facade of the kiosk and low pressure (blue) in the east-facing facade, facilitating air movement inside the building.

Fin Garden succeeds in combining a clear geometry of visible wide walkways with the intimacy of several shadowed enclosures.

below: Axonometric of the Fin Garden and buildings from the 17th and 19th centuries.

opposite top: Section axonometric view of the central kiosk. Underground canals start at the pool (the highest point in the garden) and feed into smaller fountains (at the lowest points).

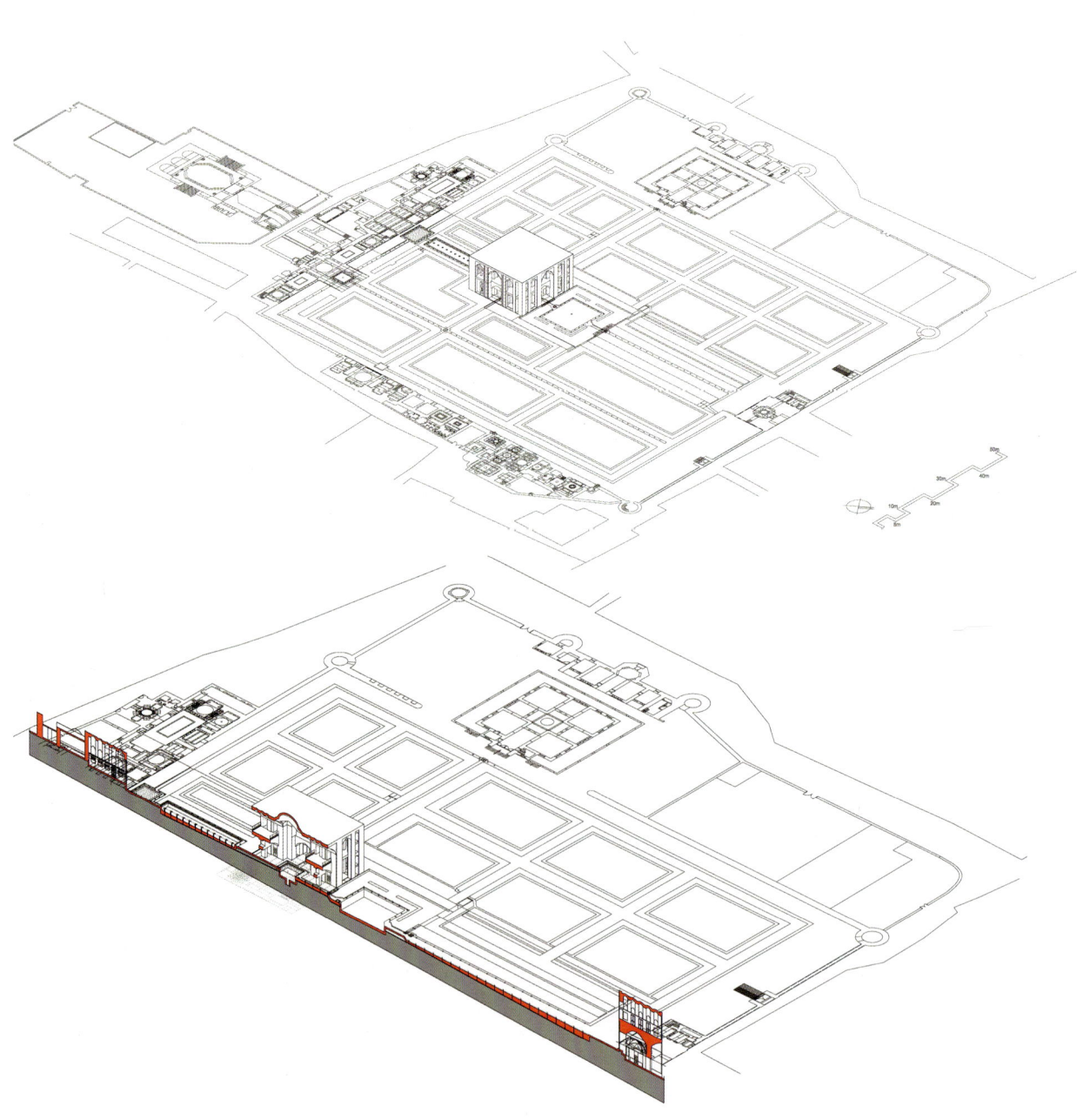

bottom: Reflected ceiling plan of the central kiosk. An intricate triangulation and meshing was required for an accurate analysis of wind behaviour, pattern and speed. The drawing shows the level of detail in the computational fluid dynamics (CFD).

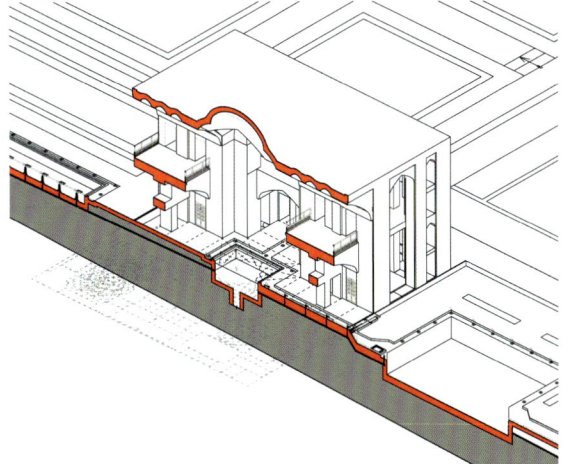
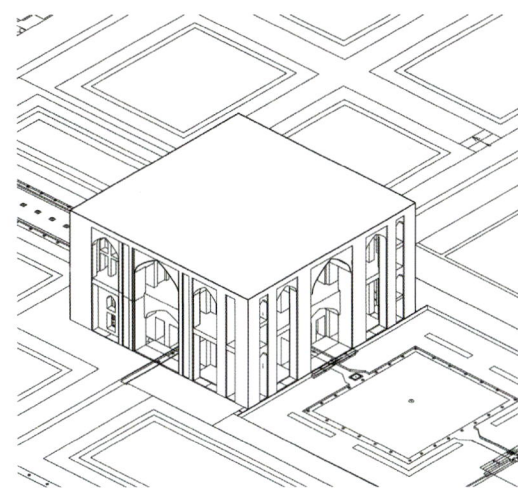

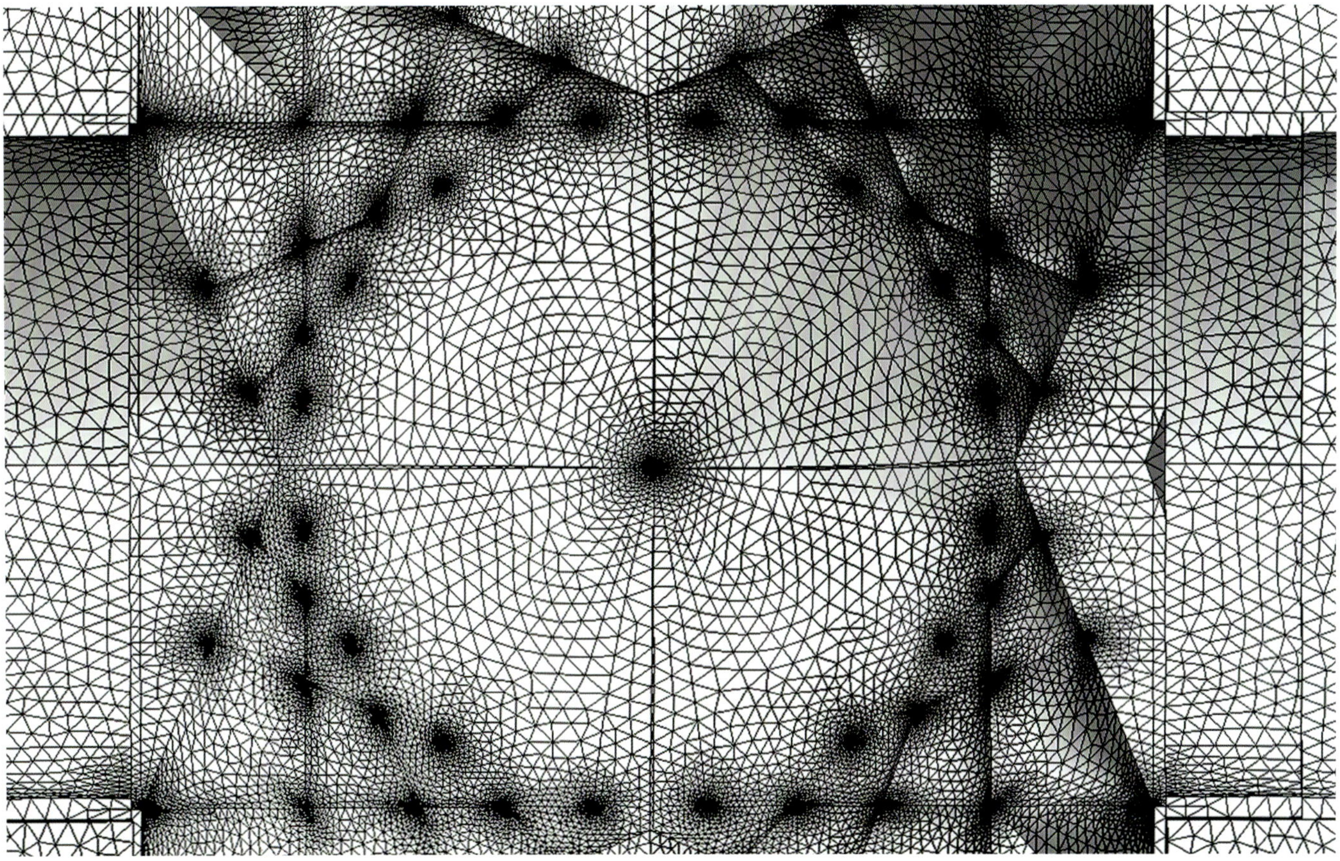

Text © 2012 John Wiley & Sons Ltd. Images: pp 38–9, 44(br), 45 © Hamidreza Jayhani; p 40 © British Library Board; p 41 © Naghshe Jahan Pars engineering consultants; pp 42, 43(tl), 44(tr) © Dr Sepehri, photos by Jassem Ghazbanpour; p 43(tr) © Nasrine Faghih; p 43(br) © Diagram redrawn by Amin Sadeghy from William R. Corliss, *Ancient Infrastructure:* *Remarkable Roads, Mines, Walls, Mounds, Stone Circles: A Catalogue of Archaeological Anomalies*, Sourcebook Project, 1999; p 44(l) © Sourced and drawn by Nasrine Faghih, completed by Hamidreza Jayhani; pp 46–51 © Sustainable Environment Association: Amin Sadeghy, Nasrine Faghih, Mehran Gharleghi and Michael Hensel

Farshad Farahi

WORLD SIMIL I

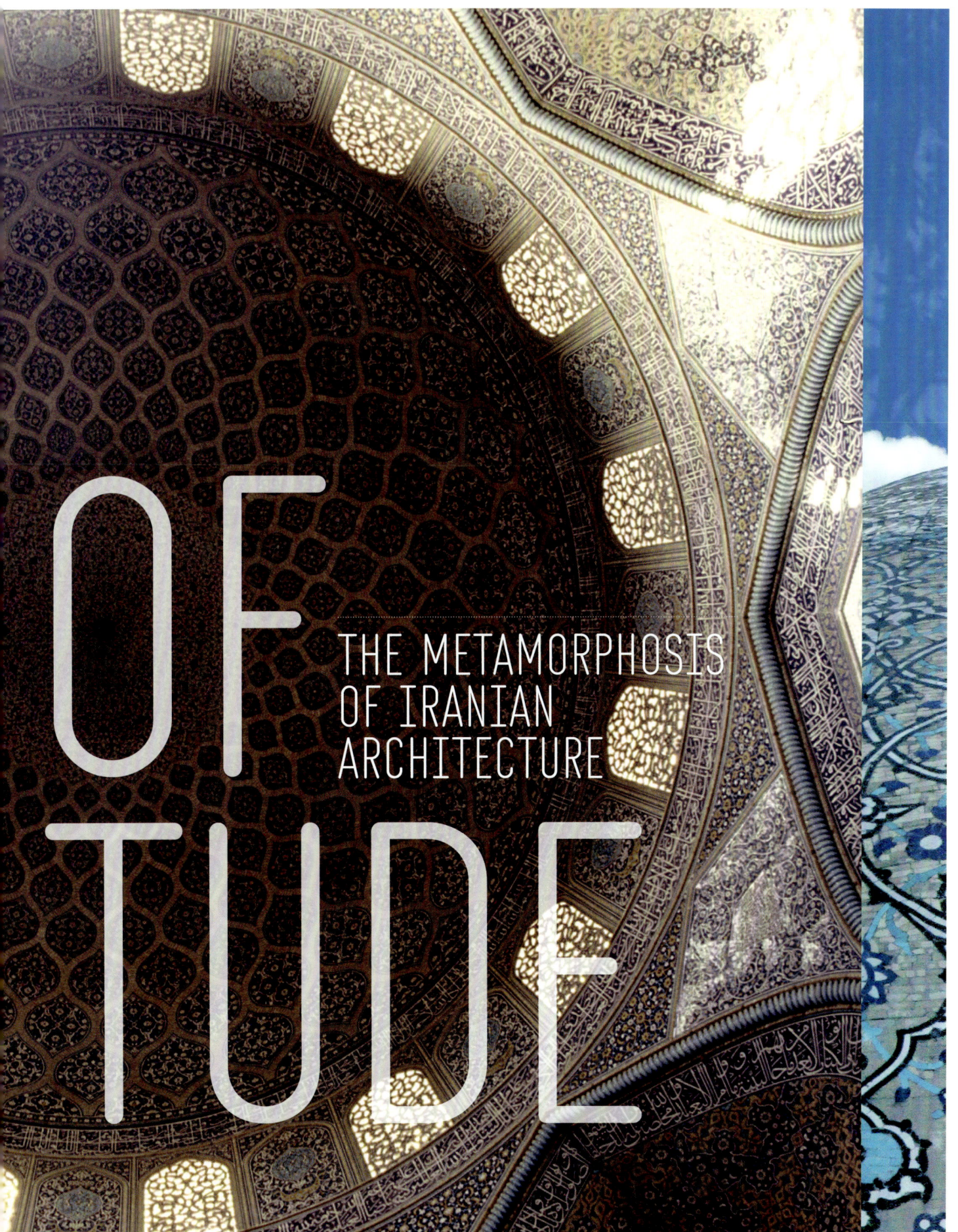

OF
TUDE

THE METAMORPHOSIS OF IRANIAN ARCHITECTURE

Sheikh Lotf-o Allah Mosque, Isfahan, Safavid period (1501–1736)
previous spread: The interior dome of the mosque. This is the most sophisticated and extraordinary ceramic work of the Safavid period. The Sheikh Lotf-o Allah Mosque is one of the main buildings in Naqsh-e Jahan Square and part of the royal family passage (axis).

How can an ancient architectural heritage become a rich resource for inspiration rather than a burden or a limitation? Moving away from a conventional formal analysis of historic architecture, which identifies particular periods with specific styles or characteristics, **Farshad Farahi** suggests an approach that unites the contemporary philosophically and spiritually with its past – by seeking out an imaginary dimension or 'World of Similitude'.

Societies with an ancient civilisation and a distinct architectural heritage often wrestle with a continuing dilemma: how to deal with, maintain and remain true to their cultural identities while simultaneously participating in global progress and modernisation. Present-day Iranian architecture is no exception. This article discusses the origin and characteristics of ancient Iranian architecture and suggests a new classification for its history. It also briefly examines contemporary developments and seeks an idea for a new Iranian architecture and its potential to impact global architecture.

The history of Iranian architecture has traditionally been approached as an archaeological subject, examining architectural characteristics associated with particular dynasties, regional historical trends or cultural watersheds such as the pre- and post-Islamic periods.[1] For the purpose of this article, Iranian architectural history is organised into four distinct periods: the Ancient period from 728 BC to AD 650; the Middle Ages from 650 to 1487; the Renaissance from 1487 to 1875, and the Modern Era from 1875 to today.[2]

The Ancient and Medieval Periods
The classical architecture of Persia began during the Ancient period with the Achaemenid (550–330 BC) dynasty and continued until the Sassanid dynasty (224–651). Its

Hasht Behesht Palace, Isfahan, Safavid period (1501–1736)
The interior ceiling of the Hasht Behesht (Eight Paradises) Palace. The pavilion of eight paradises is one of the most beautiful and exceptional applications of the ancient 'Four Arches' (*chahar tagh*) archetype.

The Gate of the Nations, Persepolis, Shiraz, Far Province, Achaemenid period (550–330 BC)
Persepolis is a transliteration of the Greek name, *perses-polis*, for 'Persian City'. Persepolis was the ceremonial capital of the Achaemenid Empire and is located 113 kilometres (70 miles) northeast of Shiraz in the Fars province of contemporary Iran. The present Persian name of Persepolis is Takht-e Jamshid, which refers to the extensive platform (*Takht*) of the Persepolis site. UNESCO declared Persepolis a World Heritage site in 1979.

Gonbad-e Qabus Tower, Gonbad-e Kavos, Golestan Province, *c* 1600
Gonbad-e Qabus is a tomb of the Sultan Qabus ibn Woshmgir. The brick-built tower is located in the centre of Gonbad-e Kavos city in Golestan province, in the northeast of Iran. At 72 metres (236 feet), it is one of the tallest pure-brick towers in the world.

maturation set the stage for the emergence and development of Iranian Middle Ages architecture, which began with the appearance of Islam in Iran. Throughout its development, Persian classical architecture maintained a gradually evolving continuity that eventually formed one of the most important schools of Islamic art and architecture – the school of Iranian Islamic art and architecture.[3] It was a period of resurgence and glamour, resulting in masterpieces of figurative art and sculptural architecture. The morphology and the subjects of Middle Ages architecture are chiefly related to religious belief and divine grace.

The architecture of the Safavid period (1501–1736) presented a new appearance that improved on the ancient classical subject matter, with values that made it in many ways true Renaissance architecture. Although the themes taken up during this period were a continuation of the themes and trends of the Ancient period, Safavid architecture fundamentally changed the relationship between functionality and artistic design. Use of pure form and dramatic structures that dominated the urban landscape communicated transcendent design born from imagination and free of structural constraints. Isfahan, the relocated and rebuilt capital of the Safavid dynasty, with a population of more than half a million citizens,[4] contains some of the most remarkable examples of Renaissance urban architecture and spaces, including the grandiose Naqsh-e Jahan Square, the largest historic square in the world and the sixth largest overall. The qualitative value of Safavid architecture can be seen in the integration of theory (philosophy) and technique (mathematics) practised in its purest form by master Sheikh Bahai (1547–1621), philosopher, mathematician and architect. The architectural themes taken up in this period constitute a sophisticated elaboration of the Ancient period, mostly concerned with the mundane, human endeavour and various aspects of life. The later development of this school of architecture is the Qajar period (1795–1925).

The evolutionary architecture of these three continuous eras spans a 2,600-year period during which spatial organisation and essential design concepts were sustained and gradually transfigured in various building types. For example, the geometrical shape of the 'Four Arches' (*chahar tagh*), consisting of a dome sitting on a square of four arches, was commonly used throughout the Sassanid period (224–651) in Zoroastrian fire temples, in the centre of which the symbolic fire burned and represented the first spiritual images of a sacred centre. It was subsequently used during the Middle Ages in the centre of 'Four Porches' (*chahar eyvane*) central courtyard architecture. There, man-made ponds covered the sacred centre with water as a symbol of the sky's mirror. In short, through time, this centre became a symbolic sacred place which man was

Naqsh-e Jahan Square, Isfahan, Safavid period (1501–1736)
View of the square from the roof of the Imam (Shah) Mosque. The spatial organisation of the square is based on a cross axis. The short axis connects Ali Qapu Palace to the Sheikh Lotf-o Allah Mosque, and previously belonged to the royal family. The longitudinal axis between the Bazar and the Imam Mosque belonged to the public. Naqsh-e Jahan Square is the centre of historical Safavid Isfahan. Its morphology uses the 'Four Porches' (*chahar eyvane*) central courtyard archetype in a new way on an urban scale.

The qualitative value of Safavid architecture can be seen in the integration of theory (philosophy) and technique (mathematics) practised in its purest form by master Sheikh Bahai (1547–1621), philosopher, mathematician and architect. The architectural themes taken up in this period constitute a sophisticated elaboration of the Ancient period, mostly concerned with the mundane, human endeavour and various aspects of life.

The architecture of the Safavid period (1501–1736) presented a new appearance that improved on the ancient classical subject matter, with values that made it in many ways true Renaissance architecture.

Although the themes taken up during this period were a continuation of the themes and trends of the Ancient period, Safavid architecture fundamentally changed the relationship between functionality and artistic design.

not permitted to enter. Through the ages, the centripetal archetype was applied to other prototypes, such as Persian gardens (*chahar bagh*), pavilions and 'four-season' houses (an ecological prototype house with components oriented based on seasonal direction and heat radiation of the sun) as well as in arts and crafts, such as in carpet designs. In each use it created an exceptional spatial organisation and coordination system that defined shapes in space, with two more dimensions oriented below (life after death) and above (symbol of entity) the centre.

The architecture of these classical periods is rooted in a theory distinguished by its belief in the existence of an independent imaginary world that intervenes between the rational and the sensory world. On one hand, this 'in between' realm takes sensory forms out of the material world, gives them an abstract and virtual determination, and 'de-materialises' them. On the other hand it gives shape, dimension and direction to the intellect and, at this level, unifies the spirit and the body. Delicate and transparent bodies such as water, mirrors and the sky are symbols of this imaginary world.[5]

This is a hermeneutic, abstract, virtual and mystical description of the imaginary world and a valuable realm of creativity, rooted in the original meaning of what ancient Persians called the 'world of similitude' (*alam-e-mesal*), which permeated Iranian architecture through the ages.

The Modern and Contemporary Periods

The Modern period in Iran was founded upon the development of Modernism and its profound influences. The process of Iran's modernisation during the Pahlavi period (1925–79) resulted in rapid urbanisation and cultural-economic changes ushered in by the appearance of new urban social classes. This has generated a false discourse of 'tradition versus modernity' that has become a challenge for Iranian contemporary art and architecture.

Contemporary Iranian architecture began in 1878 with the construction of the National Parliament building designed by Mehdi Khan Shagagi. The structure helped introduce Neoclassicism, which became a new revival style towards the end of the Qajar period. During this period and after, different Western revival styles continued to dominate Iranian architecture for more than a century.

Under Reza Shah's reign (1925–41), foreign and European-trained Iranian architects introduced early modern architecture to Iran. Among these, Gabriel Guevrekian was an internationally recognised master of the modern architectural movement and one of the companions of Le Corbusier in the Congrès Internationaux d'Architecture Moderne (CIAM).[6] Guevrekian practised in Iran for a few years, designing a number of villas and public buildings. Although his presence may have provided an opportunity for Iranians to establish an intelligent and mature modern architecture, as for example

Ali Qapu Palace, Isfahan, Safavid period (1501–1736)
previous spread: The interior ceiling of the palace. Ali Qapu was a multipurpose ceremonial palace and is located opposite the Sheikh Lotf-o Allah Mosque in Naqsh-e Jahan Square.

Reflection of a Church, Julfa, Isfahan, Safavid period (1501–1736)
Water as a mirror. Delicate and transparent bodies such as water, mirrors and the sky are symbols of the imaginary world.

Shazdeh Garden (Bagh-e Shazdeh), Mehan, Kerman Province, Qajar period (1795–1925)
The summer pavilion viewed from the garden (1850–60). With two storeys, the pavilion is located at the main entrance south of the garden. This is a characteristic example of a Persian garden.

Lucio Costa, Oscar Niemeyer and others did in Brazil, the dominance of revivalists prevented this from materialising.

The architecture of Mohammad Reza Shah's reign (1941–79) can be classified into three categories: first, early works focused on national symbols and monumental tombs of elites, including the Mausoleum of Ibn Sina in Hamadan (1951), designed by Hoshang Seyhoon, represented the continuation of the Middle Ages architecture with modern improvements; second, the international style, which began in the early 1960s, focused on urban architecture, mainly located in the capital and a few other big cities; although its building technology became trend-setting and is still in vogue, designs followed Western architecture without concern for regional design; and third, Iranian regional architecture began to take shape towards the end of Mohammad Reza Shah's reign, at which time a few thoughtful projects were created, including the Tehran Museum of Contemporary Art (1977), designed by Kamran Diba, the Azadi Monument (Tehran, 1971), designed by Hossein Amanat, and Nader Ardalan's Iranian Center for Management Studies (Tehran, 1975). Although these projects constituted progress in developing an Iranian regional architecture, this process was cut short and failed to develop.

In the early 1980s, the Postmodern architecture movement[7] coincided with the Islamic revolution of Iran and its motto of 'return to the root' that was prevalent in Iranian architecture for more than a decade. Although the social–political situation created a unique opportunity for Iranian architecture to present a new 'world of similitude' to the global architectural arena, the opportunity was lost when Iranian architects failed to create any significant internationally recognised projects.

Throughout history, interactions between space and form have been used to transform architecture in a particular era. This transformation is itself made possible with theory and technique – the tools that serve to create form and space in order to obtain an architectural language. To date, modern Iranian architecture has failed to genuinely establish and use its own theory and technique. Although it has created an impressive body of work, it has not developed the conditions that could lead to a dynamic architectural movement. Different national and international values have posed a difficulty for evaluating genuine properties of Iranian modern architecture. Indeed, having embraced Western modern architecture, modern Iranian architecture seems to have lost the 'world of similitude' that characterised Iranian architecture for thousands of years.

By the mid-1990s, the sudden and surprising appearance in Iran of Bahram Shirdel, an internationally influential architect dealing with interdisciplinary fields of architecture and science,[8] brought excitement and a new vision to Iranian architecture.[9] Shirdel came to Iran for the Imam Khomeini International Airport project and designed a contemporary

Contemporary Iranian architecture began in 1878 with the construction of the National Parliament building designed by Mehdi Khan Shagagi. The structure helped introduce Neoclassicism, which became a new revival style towards the end of the Qajar period. During this period and after, different Western revival styles continued to dominate Iranian architecture for more than a century.

Sheikh Lotf-o Allah Mosque, Isfahan, Safavid period (1501–1736)
View of the exterior dome of the mosque in Naqsh-e Jahan Square. This is one of the most innovative and skilled ceramic works of the Safavid era.

masterpiece. Although the design never materialised into the envisioned structure, it demonstrated an incredible sophistication that re-energised Iranian architecture. Shirdel currently lives and practises in Iran. He has designed a number of innovative and unique projects,[10] introducing valuable design with new theories that are entirely different from those associated with Iranian architecture to date. Although he is a target for criticism by conservatives, he has had a profound influence on the younger generation of nationally known practising architects. It appears that all important projects created after Shirdel's arrival in Iran are motivated in some capacity by his approach. In fact, his architectural prowess and international reputation make him an attractive candidate to help usher in development of a new 'world of similitude' in Iran's contemporary architecture.

The New World of Similitude

Information technology and its developments have created socioeconomic dynamics similar to those of the Industrial Revolution, in that they have opened a great gap between the highly industrially developed countries and the rest of the world. In this context the values of the architectural heritage of different countries can now either become an active part of new movements and viewpoints of global architecture, or lose their durability and relevance and become mere followers. To deal with the complexity and pluralism of the latter is not only a challenge, but also an opportunity to offer a view and a vision that does not belong to any specific culture or civilisation, but that could be utilised by all societies. Since architecture deals with new spaces configured by new forms, creative architecture can take any matter and proceed through imagination to arrive at an abstract view bearing no apparent resemblance to the starting point. In fact, anything could be an incentive to animate the creative functioning of an active mind going beyond the boundaries of tangible and visible objects in an abstract manner. Having such a vision, one cannot prescribe a single method of designing and a unique solution for each specific design.

The wealth of today's Iranian architecture consists of two groups of practitioners: on one hand, outstanding internationally recognised Iranians with a considerable theoretical background and knowledge of contemporary architecture; on the other, a wide range of national architects with diverse regional experience. Daryush Shayegan, the great Iranian philosopher, stated that the hypertextual dialogue 'has one foot in prehistory's culture and the other in the metamorphosis of the future'.[11] At no other point in Iranian or Persian history have the practitioners of Iranian architecture had the opportunity to engage in the level of hypertextual dialogue necessary to spawn an architectural movement with the potential for a truly global impact.

Hossein Amanat, Azadi Monument, Tehran, 1971
Previously known as the Shahyad Tower but today renamed the Azadi Monument, Amanat's creation is the symbol of Tehran and the gateway to Iran's modern capital city. Located in the Azadi Square, today it functions as an urban space for national and political events and demonstrations.

Iranian architecture, enabled by information technology and global communication, has created an environment where different layers of meaning formed through the architectural metamorphosis from ancient times until today can finally coalesce into a world of different meaning and imagination beyond the limited insights of contemporary Iranian architecture. With focused vision and effective communication, the Iranian architectural community will be able to impact global architecture, and relative proportional abilities will transfigure themselves as a hermeneutic area of insight, opening up the possibility for a hypertextual dialogue between different worldviews and creating a 'new world of similitude'. 𝔻

Notes

1. Arthur Upham Pope, *Introducing Persian Architecture*, Oxford University Press (London), 1971.
2. See Farshad Farahi, 'A Brief Survey on Iranian History of Architecture', *Iranian A&U magazine* 50–51, Spring 1999.
3. Mohammad Karim Pirnia, *Iranian Architectural Trends*, Islamic Art Publisher Institution (Tehran), 1990.
4. Jean Chardin, *Travel in Iran*, London, 1686, trans Hussein Arizi, Negah Publisher (Tehran), 1983.
5. Daryush Shayegan, *Idols of the Mind*, Amir Kabir Publisher (Tehran), 1976. An interpretation of Iranian philosophy as articulated by Henry Corbin and Daryush Shayegan.
6. Eric Mumford, *The CIAM Discourse on Urbanism*, MIT Press (Cambridge, MA), 1958. The first meeting of CIAM in Paris was organised by Le Corbusier and Guevrekian.
7. Charles Jencks, *Post-Modernism*, Academy Editions (London), 1987.
8. Giuseppa Di Cristina, 𝔻 *Architecture and Science*, 2001.
9. Greg Lynn, 𝔻 *Folding In Architecture*, No 63, Profile 102, March/April 1993.
10. Ramin Safari Rad, *Sharestan* 15-16, Special Issue on Bahram Shirdel, Spring/Summer 2007.
11. Daryush Shayegan, 'Merging of Horizons: A Letter to the Younger Generation', *Iranian A&U magazine* 60–61, February 2001.

Kamran Diba, Tehran Museum of Contemporary Art, Tehran, 1977
The museum is one of the masterpieces of 1970s Iranian architecture and constituted progress in developing a distinguished Iranian regional architecture.

Abstract Reflection of a Dialogue
top: Abstract image of an environment in which different layers of meaning are formed through architectural metamorphosis from ancient times until today.

Text © 2012 John Wiley & Sons Ltd. Images: pp 52–3 (background), 58, 59(l), 61(t) © Fatemeh Dadkhah; pp 52–3, 54–7, 58(r), 60, 61(b) © Kamran Adle

Reza Daneshmir and Catherine Spiridonoff

SUBTERR
LANDSCA

THE FAR-REACHING INFLUENCE OF THE UNDERGROUND QANAT NETWORK IN ANCIENT AND PRESENT-DAY IRAN

Persia's ancient civilisation was constructed on qanats – an extensive subterranean network of canals – that supplied vital water for drinking and irrigation. **Reza Daneshmir and Catherine Spiridonoff of Fluid Motion Architects** describe how an on-site encounter with qanats in Tehran helped to unleash not only a new understanding of historic urban development and its social fabric, which evolved around these ancient water channels, but also led to new thinking about the current potential of the qanats and their possibilities for greening the capital.

ANEAN
PE

Qanat Map of Tehran
With more than 600 qanats, Tehran has the potential for the creation of new urban spaces.

Fluid Motion Architects (FMA) was recently involved in the design and execution of a project in Tehran that required the excavation of the site, during which came the discovery of two qanats: ancient Persian water networks that tap into underground mountain water sources. These subterranean water canals were gushing out such a large amount of water that they actually brought the excavations to a halt. In order to solve the problem, FMA consulted one of Tehran's main qanat experts, Ahmad Maleki, with whom the firm collaborated for three months on a plan to divert the qanats. This introduction to the qanat network proved an invaluable experience. It not only provided knowledge of their organisation and construction, but also a much more far-reaching understanding of the extent of their influence on ancient Persian cities and the possibilities they hold for today's urban development.

Invented 3,000 years ago by the ancient Persians, the qanat is a hydraulic structure. Employing gravitational force, it can extract groundwater without consuming any energy. There are 50,000 qanats in Iran, 600 of which, with a total length of 2,000 kilometres (1,243 miles), are in Tehran. Dating back 700 years, Mehrgerd is the oldest existing qanat in the capital. Bastani Parizi described in his preface to *Qanat in Iran* (2005) how all the largest cities in ancient Iran were riddled with qanats; even those such as Tabriz, for instance, that had a river and relatively high rainfall.[1] Parizi proceeded to explain how this legacy could be fully tapped into today. The Alborz mountain range, for instance, which is one of the largest water resources in Iran, has the potential, if the rivers, streams and valleys radiating through it could be integrated into an engineered plan to support new settlements. It could be possible to have around a hundred cities of a million inhabitants in a 1,000-kilometre (621-mile) range, from Khorasan in the northeast to Azerbaijan in the northwest. By fully utilising the Alborz's snow and glacier melting water, sufficient crops could be cultivated on the Alborz range to feed as many as 100 million people.

The role of the qanat in providing not only the technical means of supporting Persia's ancient civilisation with a ready supply of water for drinking and irrigation, but also in assisting in the creation of a rich and diverse culture, is highlighted by Mohammad Hossein Papoli Yazdi in his book *The Quassabeh Qanat of Gonabad*.[2] He points out that if qanats had not been invented some 3,000 years ago, large villages and cities would not have developed, and agriculture, industry and trade would not have evolved across some of the most arid and semi-arid regions of the earth, particularly in Asia and southern Africa. In areas with low rainfall and no spring water, sustainable life would have been impossible without groundwater and the qanat system.

Furthermore, the qanat network had an even more far-reaching impact, directly informing the structural urban fabric and affecting the social fabric. In the cities that were supplied by qanat water, it was impossible for both the rich and the poor to live far from qanat aqueducts. All would therefore settle in the same neighbourhood, along the qanat network, and use the same mosque, bazaar, bathhouse and *zourkhaneh* (a place for traditional Persian sports) and, as a result, interacted directly face to face on an everyday basis. Yazdi concludes by asserting the qanat as the main influencing force

Fluid Motion Architects, Mellat Bank Office Tower, Tehran, 2011
Cutting off the historic infrastructure of a qanat during the excavation of a project under construction. In recent years, with the increase in large-scale projects in Tehran, and the need for great amounts of excavation for solving parking requirements, such occurrences have become commonplace.

Kerman, 1955
bottom: The fabric of this historic Iranian city is fluid, undulated, and probably formed according to the underground network of qanats.

The Ancient Quassabeh Qanat, Gonabad, 1000 BC
below: At more than 3,000 years old, and a depth of 340 metres (1,115 feet), this is Iran's oldest, deepest qanat.

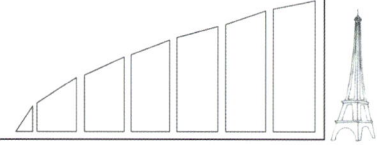

'in the foundation of urbanization, civilization, and agriculture in extensive parts of plains and mountainsides on the earth'.[3]

Revealing a New Urban Topology

For many years the formal geometries of ancient monuments, like the palaces, castles and grand mosques at Yazd and Isfahan, for example, seemed entirely at odds with the wider urban fabric that appeared fluid, dynamic and even illogical.

From time to time, this urban flow even unexpectedly changed its direction; a shift that accorded neither with the geographical directions nor with the direction of the Kiblah (Kaaba in Mecca). This flow surrounds both modest structures such as houses, and larger and more prominent public buildings and monuments (the beauty of this integration is that the geometric structures and large plazas float in the whole fluid flow of the city). Moreover, over the last 50 years studies of Iran's ancient cities by distinguished contemporary Iranian architects and prominent non-Iranian researchers have constantly overlooked this fluid and dynamic flow. Analysis of the Iranian city has remained focused on the palaces, bazaars, and public or religious buildings. The understanding of Iranian architecture has been limited entirely to this perception of architectural structures as having regular and symmetrical geometry, details and motifs. The organisation of the urban fabric has been assessed in only the vaguest terms or been regarded as somewhat haphazard: broken or destroyed to widen paths, in the course of city development and current constructions. Only valuable buildings of the urban fabric have been preserved or frozen, in the hope that they will bring a touch of the past to new streets. The key question remains unanswered: what is the underlying structure of the ancient cities of Iran? In arid and semi-arid regions of Iran, could it be the qanats that provide the topological structure of the ancient urban fabric?

Looking at the first series of aerial photographs taken of Iranian cities in the 1950s, the fluid flow of urban fabric is absolutely evident, as are the points at which it is severed and transformed to voids by regular Cartesian grids of newly built streets. If we follow the fluid structural lines of cell-like houses, the old city appears. This condition could be regarded as an ideal solution for restoring the old damaged fabric and replacing it with Modern architecture to attain a harmonious and efficient combination, upholding the complexity and spatial depth of the existing city fabric.

Unfortunately, qanat maps of all of Iran's historic cities are yet to be generated. So it cannot be precisely determined what is happening beneath the cities' undulating surfaces and which paths the qanats run through. The only existing map is for the qanats network of Tehran, which contains some defects and ambiguities. But based on this map, produced by water systems experts, the logic of the relationship between the subterranean qanat systems, gardens, courtyards and generally green spaces on the surface of Tehran city is absolutely clear. As an example, a part of Sangelaj old qanat and the large green spaces connected to it, from Daneshjou Park to Shahr Park, and their peripheral residential fabric are displayed. These maps and diagrams show that the qanat structure links large and small pieces of gardens and courtyards like a thread and with its flexible and

Periphery of Sangelaj Qanat and its related gardens, Tehran, 1750
Image showing the position of Iranian gardens in relation to the underground qanat network.

Historical Fabric of Iran
In a most general way, Iranian cities can be described as a series of lines and points, where the qanats are the lines, and the gardens the points.

Fault Lines Map of Iran
Fault line map in accordance with the position of the prominent mountains of the region.

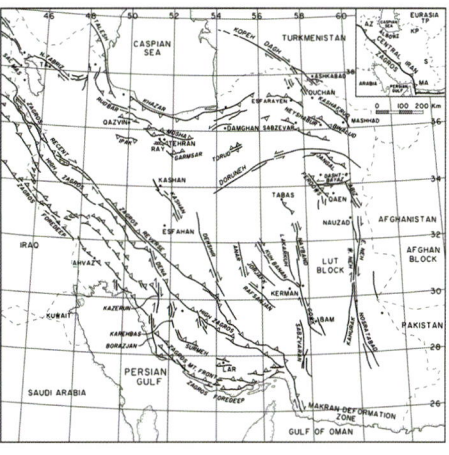

Darakeh River Valley (Chamran Expressway to the north of Tehran)
One of the five river valleys radiating from the northern mountains of Tehran, which with the construction of the expressway is being used as a vehicular circulation route instead of a public urban space.

Tehran is the eighth most polluted city in the world, and the number of days that air pollution has crossed the risk border in the cold season has amounted to more than a month. This has made it uncomfortable to live in the city during the day and has caused serious dangers to the health of children and the elderly.

fluid geometry that indicates groundwater flow systems, it has formed fluid and complex structures of buildings on the ground. This system, which was based on the organic movement of the groundwater, had developed the spatial character of city architecture in Iran before the establishment of Tehran's modern water piping systems in 1955. Another important fact is that the plateau of Iran is an earthquake-prone region and this vast area is formed by a collection of tectonic plates, which are distinguished from each other by fault lines.

The natural structure of fault lines in the historical cities of Iran on the one hand, and the man-made qanat networks on the other, are the two hidden topological systems under the visible layer of cities that are linked together. For instance, the relationship between the geographical location of Tehran and the northern foothills can be regarded as tripartite: first, it was dictated by its proximity to the mountains, which accumulated an adequate amount of snow in the highlands in the winter (see A in the diagram bottom right); second, it was determined by the fault and fracture lines that border the mountains and plains and enable snow water to penetrate deeply into the earth (B); and third, the city's position in relation to the mountains was governed by the gradient of the mountain range, which is about 10 per cent, gradually decreasing as one moves away from the mountain (C).

Iranian architects then designed a system of aqueducts under the surface of the ground with regard to the underground water tables that were stored naturally below the earth's crust. They used the qanat networks structure (D) gravitational force and the natural slope of land to supply water to the ground's surface and create the required gardens and green spaces for cities and residential areas.

In the second half of the 20th century, with the construction of the modern system of tap water and drilling deep wells, this organic and sustainable system was ignored and gradually forgotten. In all of Tehran's comprehensive urban plans in the past 50 years, these valuable structures under the city's surface have remained neglected.

After the revolution in Iran, Tehran's rapid expansion and numerous constructions have led these priceless structures to be cut, occluded or desiccated in the construction process whenever a new building, expressway or, more recently, subway lines meet a qanat's paths. Fortunately, in the northern and central parts of the city, there are still many active qanats. Tehran's big blobs of green space like the Abbasabad Hills, Taleghani Park and Pardisan Park remain irrigated by these qanats for free.

Greening Tehran

Today, Tehran suffers from a shortage of urban open spaces, such as squares and plazas. The parks and sidewalks of the main streets comprise the major public spaces, and are insufficient considering the size of the city. An uncontrolled increase in the number of cars and buildings in the past two decades (since the Iran–Iraq war), heavy traffic and air pollution have not only affected and faded the experience of walking in the city, but have also transformed Tehran to a dense city that lacks properly proportioned spaces.

In the latest masterplan for Tehran, in 2006, a system

Seismic Hazard Assesment of Iran
The Iranian plateau consists of tectonic planes created by the geographical position of mountains and flats.

Schematic Section of Tehran
Image indicating the relationship between the fabric, mountains and fault lines of Tehran.

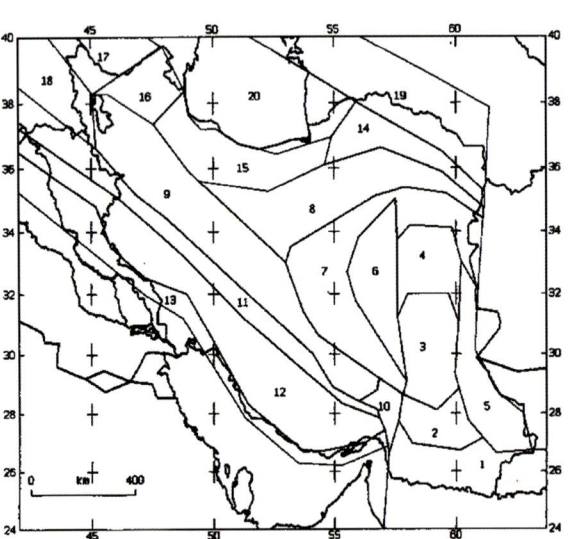

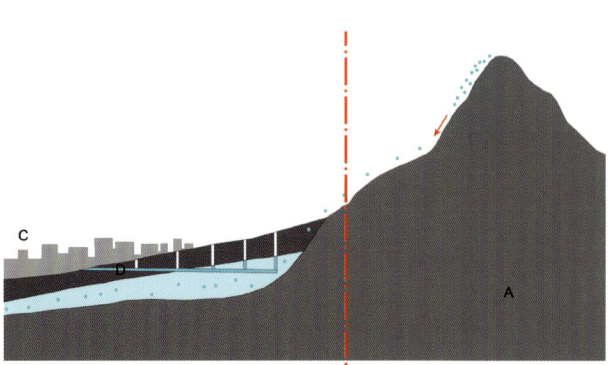

of green spaces had been designated using five river valleys radiating from the mountains to the north of the city. Unfortunately, with the construction of new expressways, these areas are now dominated by cars; they can therefore only be seen from inside a car and there is no possibility for the public to experience these spaces as parks or properly maintained leisure areas. Excessive development in recent years, particularly in the northern parts of the city, has resulted in a loss of gardens and valuable green spaces and has transformed them into compact high-rise buildings.

Tehran is the eighth most polluted city in the world, and the number of days that air pollution has crossed the risk border in the cold season has amounted to more than a month. This has made it uncomfortable to live in the city during the day and has caused serious dangers to the health of children and the elderly. Using the existing qanat structures underneath Tehran's surface and the new subway system, it is possible to imagine an underground city where the weather and environmental conditions are controlled and which provides a place for people during months when air pollution is unbearable. The idea of an underground garden city is reminiscent of the ancient structure of Tehran, described by travellers and historians as an underground city with many gardens. In 1009, the traveller Ebn-e-Houghol Moahamad Baghdadi described Tehran as a village in the north of Rey city with many gardens and a variety of fruits, and mentions that the deviants of Tehran whose profession was robbery lived underground. In 1203, Shahab-e-din Yaghout Hemavi describes Tehran as a large village with underground houses.

Subterranean Tehran could first be constructed in scattered patches, and in some appropriate places of the city built structures on the ground level and their active functions moved underground. The remaining ground could be changed into a garden. An increase in usable land surface and the propagation of underground urban patches would increase the amount of green spaces on the ground level. Little by little Tehran would transform into a garden city once again.

Undulant walkways could be created along qanat routes linking new gardens to one another. To achieve this, a number of paths would need to be identified and the buildings along those paths, those without any specific architectural value, purchased and redesigned. It would then be possible to enjoy walking in Tehran and to enjoy the city from a new perspective; an experience that has been forgotten in recent years. A garden city for walkers inside hectic Tehran conjures up the idea of expressways being replaced by walkways. A set of paths along a series of underground gardens could be an alternative to jammed streets.

In conclusion, as the Iranian plateau is located in a hot and arid region, the invention of qanats as a system for managing underground water was a crucial factor in the development of urban life in this area. The most important historic Iranian cities were formed based on these principles, and thus their future growth is also dependent on serious consideration of the use of qanats. Their importance, in addition to their role as a system of water management, is their topology and fluid structure that has the potential for creating dynamic, mysterious spaces, such as those of ancient Iran. ⌂

Masterplan of River Valleys, Tehran, 2006
Tehran's river valleys are its main green spaces.

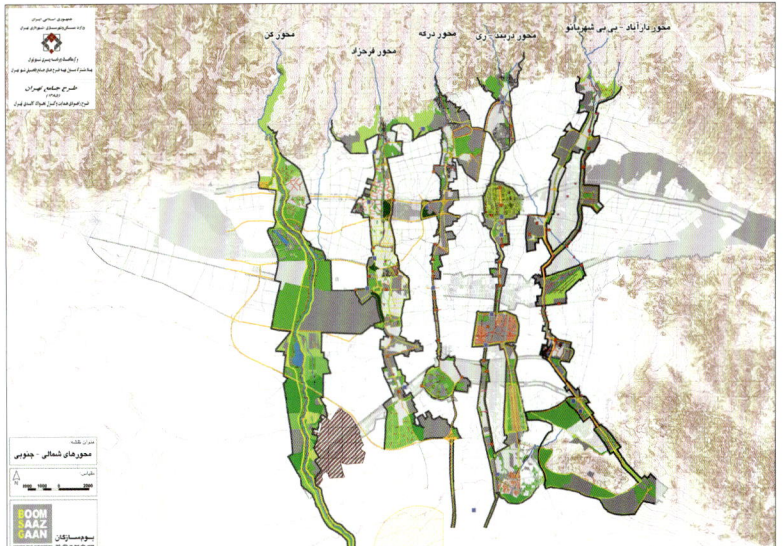

Notes
1. Ahmad Maleki and Ahmad Khorsandi Aghaee, *Qanat in Iran: The Case Study of Tehran Qanats*, Urban Planning Press (Tehran), 2005, pp 3, 7.
2. Mohammad Hossein Papoli Yazdi, *The Quassabeh Qanat in Gonabad*, Khorasan Water Department Press (Tehran), 2000, pp 9, 235.
3. Ibid.

Text © 2012 John Wiley & Sons Ltd. Images; pp 62–3, 64(l & tr), 65(c), 66–7, 68(r) © Fluid Motion Architects pp 64(br), 65(l) © National Cartographic Center (NCC); pp 65(r), 68(l) © International Institute of Earthquake Engineering and Seismology p 69 © Pars Boom Architects

Darab Diba

CONTEMPORARY ARCHITECTURE

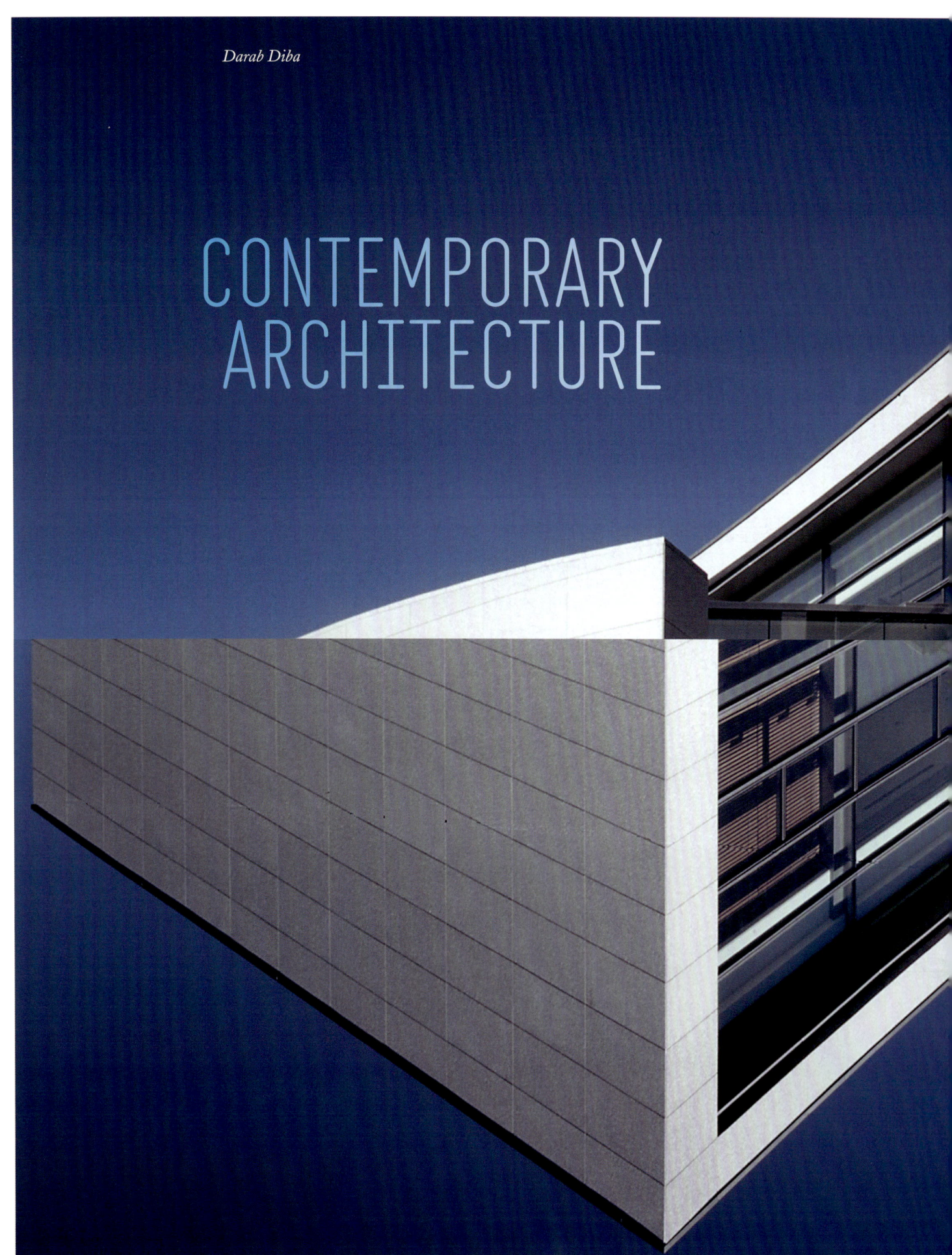

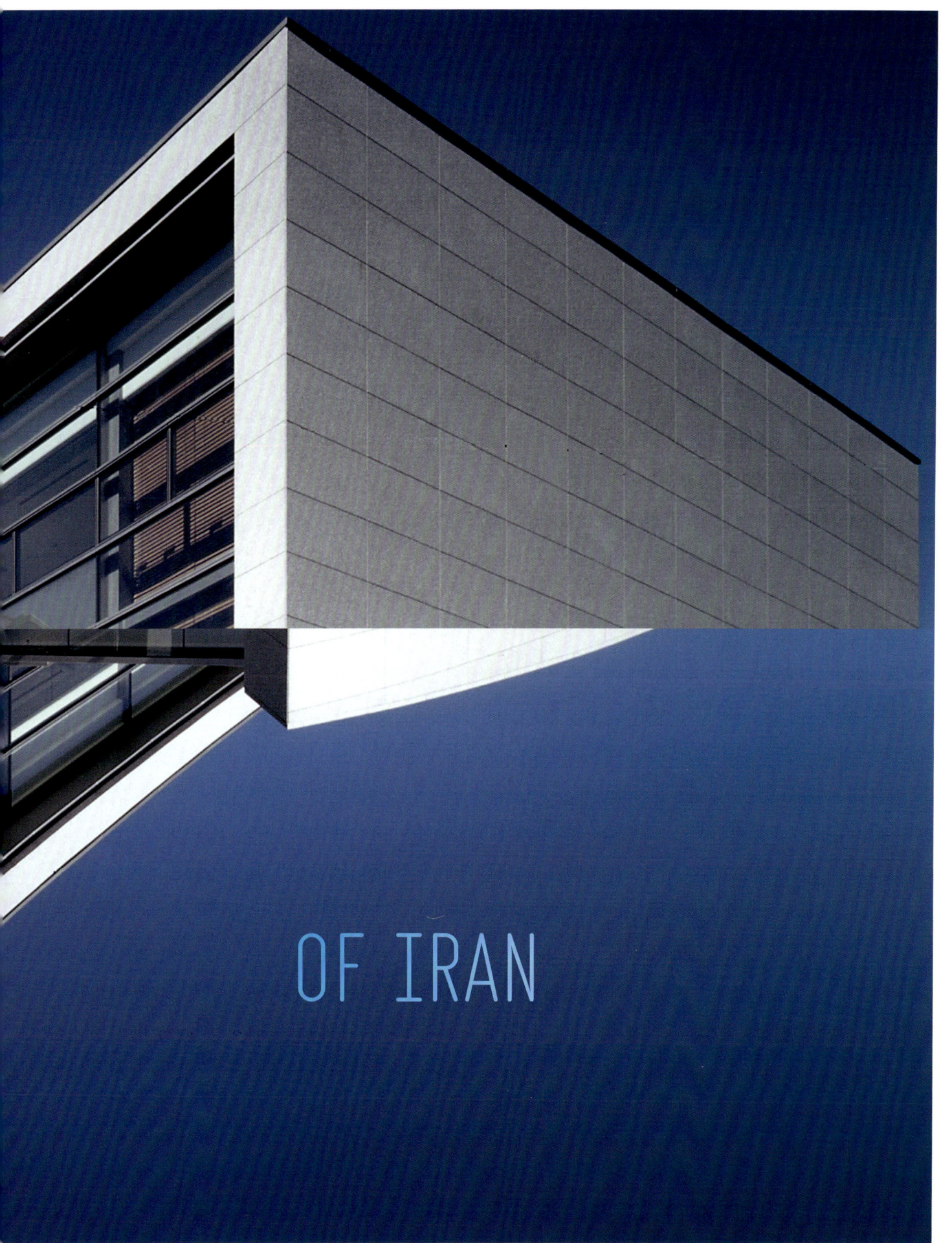

OF IRAN

Notions of identity, culture, tradition and history are key to understanding the contemporary architecture of Iran. **Darab Diba** explains how the establishment of the Islamic Republic of Iran in 1979 broke with an approach that for almost two centuries had directly equated modernity with Western influence. A revival of interest in Iran's own 'Iran-ness' initially manifested itself in a retrospective interest in historic styles, but has more recently shifted into a sophisticated appreciation of the essence of the country's heritage.

To fully understand and evaluate contemporary architecture in Iran requires a study that goes beyond the analysis of a discipline in which numerous political and social interferences have taken place over the years and, in so doing, brings to the fore the present history of this country.[1] It is key here to consider notions of identity, culture, tradition and history.[2] Since modern times, Iran, whose culture is essentially based on Islam and its associated metaphysical concepts, has been confronted with new Western values:[3] scientism, rationalism and the economic considerations of world geopolitics. Ancient trade routes meant that for many centuries there had been a largely open and even exchange between Iran, its neighbours and southern European countries. In the 19th century, though, this was disrupted by the colonial aspirations of Britain and other Western powers in the Middle East and Asia. This led to an entirely new level of cultural hegemony in which the Western worldview was advocated and imposed as the most 'advanced' or modern.

This historically led to an erosion and disintegration of traditional forms and customs.

This article will look at the influence of Western culture on Iranian architecture in the modern period and how it has been readdressed in the last few decades with the establishment of the Islamic Republic of Iran: through a revival of interest in Iran's own 'Iran-ness', which initially manifested itself in an interest in historic forms and elements, but has more recently developed into a sophisticated appreciation of the essence of the country's heritage.

THE QAJAR PERIOD (1795–1925)

Iran's confrontation with Western civilisation that began with the Qajar dynasty brought political and social modernisation during the period stretching from roughly 1800 to the middle of the 20th century. This upheaval naturally engendered a transformation in architecture and, eventually, the rise of a novel eclectic architecture in Iran.

It would not be far-fetched to say that until the beginning of the rule of Naser al-Din Shah in 1848, most of the buildings were traditional, but during his 48-year reign, a transformation took place in the field of architecture. It was clearly due to the infatuation with the West and was manifested most prominently in palaces and monuments. Modernity in Persian architecture developed under the influence of the Classicism of the Western world. This interaction was demonstrated in classical plans, layouts, openings, entrances, roofs, and the use of symmetrical spaces mingled with some traditional Iranian configurations in windows, elevations, decorations and the use of brick.

THE PAHLAVI DYNASTY
Reza Shah (1925–41)
It was during Reza Shah's rule that the industrialisation of the country began to take place. The first 10 years were a period of innovation and bold measures, changes and modernisation.[4] Road and rail networks

Kamran Diba, Tehran Museum of Contemporary Art, Tehran, 1977
The museum projects a clear reference to classical Iranian architecture with pure volumes and the use of desert windcatchers (*badgir*) in a metaphoric urban landmark.

Houshang Seyhoun, Mausoleum of Ibn Sina (Avicenna), Hamadan, 1952
opposite top: An important example of a mausoleum design with formal references, which functions as a booster of national pride based on Ibn Sina scientific and cultural representation.

Shahabeddin Arfaei, Persian Gulf Museum of Anthropology, Bandar Abbas, 2004
The design reflects and resumes local typologies and the hot and humid climate of Bandar Abbas.

were built in conjunction with a marked Europeanisation of social behaviour. New materials such as steel, cement, concrete and glass were employed in the new constructions, and new building types such as railway stations, factories, cinemas, hospitals, office and public buildings, governmental institutions, ministries, universities and banks as well as roads and infrastructures were implemented.

Another approach was to resume iconic archaeological monuments of the past to create the important public and governmental buildings of the new era. It was also influenced by 19th-century Neoclassical European buildings. The gateways of Meydan-e Mashgh, Toopkhaneh Square and Hassan Abad Square in Tehran are examples of this trend.

Among the most notable buildings were the National Bank (Bank Melli), the Ministry of Foreign Affairs, the Ministry of Justice, the Officers Club, the Sports Stadium, the Central Post Office, the Ghavam Saltaneh house (Abgineh Museum), as well as different buildings of Tehran University's campus. Some of the most influential architects of these times, Karim Tahirzadeh Bihzad, Mohsen Foroughi, Vartan Hovanesian, Ali Sadegh, Kayghobad Zafar Bakhtiar, Paul Abkar, Gabriel Guevrekian and Iraj Moshiri were proponents of Modernism. In the same period, André Godard designed, with Maxime Siroux, the Iran Bastan Museum, a good example of architectural fusion between modern technologies and traditional Iranian architecture.

Mohammad Reza Shah (1941–79)

Mohammad Reza Pahlavi rose to power in 1941. During his reign, two major and overlapping trends can be discerned: the development of the school of Modernism, and the dialogue between tradition and Modernism.[5]

Numerous government and commercial buildings like the Senate, now the Islamic parliament, the Ministry of Oil and the Behshahr complex were erected under the influence of advanced international Modernism by prominent architects such as Mohsen Foroughi, Heydar Ghiai and Abdolaziz Farmanfarmaian.

This distinct presence of International Modernism continued until 1979, and we can see its influence in buildings such as the Takhti (Amjadieh) Stadium, the City Theatre, the Azadi Sports Compound and the Ministry of Agriculture, all designed by reputable architects such as Jahanguir Darvish, Manoutcher Moghtader, Ali Sardar Afkhami and Abdolaziz Farmanfarmaian.

Other architects such as Houshang Seyhoun, Nader Ardalan, Hossein Amanat and Kamran Diba tried to achieve a cultural identity in Iranian architecture. These four architects made a serious attempt to fuse Iranian classical heritage into new vocabularies and present technologies. Efforts to achieve a cultural identity in Iranian architecture advanced through their works. By designing tombs for famous scientific and

Nader Ardalan, Iran Center for Management Studies (Imam Sadegh University), Tehran, 1975
This project integrated the Business School curriculum with a contemporary interpretation of the classic Paradise Garden, straight axes, hierarchical spaces, and the traditional madrasa plan in a brick architectural expression.

Darab Diba, Embassy of Iran in Berlin, Berlin, 2003
The design follows a traditional Iranian typology and spatial configuration with the use of concrete and white stone.

literary figures, like Avicenna's tomb in the city of Hamadan, or Khayyám's tomb in the city of Neyshabur, Houshang Seyhoun was one of the important architects during this period. Paying attention to pure geometrical volumes he achieved metaphoric expression, innovative and creative design where forms and materials such as stone, brick, steel and concrete were used in new combinations.

Hossein Amanat, following Seyhoun's path and direction, soon became an architect of note with buildings like the complex of the Cultural Heritage Organization where essential Iranian typologies and improved local materials were used through new expressions. Linking a strong geometry, referential axes, courtyard and subtle related use of concrete and brick, he achieved valuable realisations. However, the outstanding work of Amanat remains the Shahyad monument (1971) built to represent the Persian civilisation and culture, which forms a symbolic entrance complex for Tehran. Renamed Azadi (Liberty) Square after the revolution, the monument has become the most significant icon of the country and an active plaza for celebrations, parades, cultural events and activities.

In this period new discourses were gradually introduced through the presence of individuals like Nader Ardalan and Kamran Diba in which history and tradition were considered as indispensable parts of the Iranian architectural identity. Ardalan's research for the book *The Sense of Unity*[6] was also influential and, as a result, some exemplary buildings related to this trend came into existence, such as the Iran Center for Management Studies (today the Imam Sadegh University), which was inspired by universal principles and makes reference to a specifically Iranian relationship of space with nature. Diba, with the design of the new city of Shushtar, Niavaran Cultural Center, Jondi Shapour University and the Tehran Museum of Contemporary Art (1977) achieved an essential dialogue between Iranian cultural heritage and present times.

The Tehran Museum of Contemporary Art employs introversion in its principles of organisation, and the design of spatial elements, with tall light-wells reminiscent of desert windcatchers, is a clear reference to Iranian architecture. The design of the Shushtar residential compounds is based on the principles of organisation and typology of traditional Iranian cities and the use of local materials adjusted to the climate.

THE ISLAMIC REPUBLIC

The Iranian revolution of 1979 was a watershed and a major turning point in the country's views, values and politics. It put an end to a period of unbridled modernisation and, in its initial phase, sought to dismantle everything dating from the Shah's time.[7] The revolution intensified anti-Western values as it invigorated Islamist challenges to the authority of secular states, and encouraged a radical social change, rooted among the people and organised around an Islamic ideology.[8]

> *The Iranian revolution of 1979 was a watershed and a major turning point in the country's views, values and politics. It put an end to a period of unbridled modernisation and, in its initial phase, sought to dismantle everything dating from the Shah's time.*

Behrouz Ahmadi, Main Administration Building of Bam, Bam, 2007
The design was influenced and conceptualised by Iranian classical typology, with a centralised courtyard, rhythmic arcades and the use of brick.

Farhad Ahmadi, International Isfahan Cultural Center, Isfahan, 2006
opposite top right: View through the main entrance of the cultural centre, which is defined by strong axes and geometrical archetypal configurations.

Iraj Kalantari, Embassy of Iran in Tbilisi, Georgia, 2006
A cubic volumetric design with interior reflections and functional flexibility.

The Housing Foundation became effective in giving shelter to the most deprived. The Ministry of the Interior provided drinking water and electricity to the villages and smaller settlements. Popular self-made development organisations like the Djahad-e Sazandegi and the Bassidj came into operation to improve people's living conditions, and piped water, health services, electricity and schools were introduced even in some of the most remote districts.

During the 1980s and 1990s, efforts to rejuvenate Islamic culture were given priority. The use of materials like brick and tiles, and ornamental elements like moulding and calligraphy, were intended to give an Islamic spirit to buildings. The shrine of Imam Khomeini, the Organization of the Hajj, and the Sharif University Mosque in Tehran are distinct examples of this style. It is, however, reasonable to say that this trend, essentially an imitation of past patterns and forms detached from time and place, cannot have a lasting place in contemporary Iranian architecture.

In the meantime, an eclectic architecture influenced by that of the West came into existence with a number of architects taking elements of Iranian architecture and combining them with Western Postmodernism: historical motifs, traditional styles, cultural symbolism, eclecticism and other trends of the 20th century. Architectural elements from both cultures were applied to facades and plans with generally orderly geometrical forms and systems.

Other Iranian architects attempted to lead their designs towards an appropriated identity based on Iran's architectural heritage.[9] These two major influences engendered works that displayed some Modernist tastes and themes as well as elements taken from Islamic or traditional Iranian architecture. The Bureau for Members of Parliament, the Allame Dehkhoda University in Qazvin, the Honarestan of Karaj, the Pasteur Institute and the dormitories of the University of Yazd are often-cited examples of this trend. Sometimes these structures included the repetition of traditional Iranian elements like arches, windcatchers, domes and half-domes and variations in brickwork next to space frames. As such they were attempts to create a variegated and Iranian spirit, but at the cost of some eclectic fusion. In this category are the Armita office tower by Behrouz Ahmadi and the Rafsanjan Sport Complex by Hadi Mirmiran (see Saman Sayar's article on the work of Mirmiran on pp 80–7).

In national competitions, Mirmiran's National Academies of the Islamic Republic of Iran (1994) was a milestone in Iran's architectural platform. The construction of Iranian embassies around the world is another important event of the last decade. The goal was to translate Iran's perennial heritage into a contemporary vocabulary, creating archetypes and a timeless identity. In this respect, works were designed in which

Hossein Sheikh Zeineddin, Embassy of Iran in Tokyo, Tokyo, 2004
right and pp 70–1: The two-fold interconnected volume links a close exterior envelope through an interior spatial transparency.

Hossein Amanat, Azadi Square (formerly Shahyad Square), Tehran, 1971
The Shahyad monument was built to represent the Persian civilisation and culture, soon to become the most important symbolic icon of the country.

Hooman Balazadeh, Shahkaram Office and Commercial Building, Karaj, 2007
A volumetric varied play of cubes with different night and day expressions, each representing an office quarter.

Defining the exact position of today's Iranian architecture elicits various points of view. The increasing importance of literature related to linguistic philosophy, Post-Constructivism, Structuralism, Deconstruction, semiotics, globalisation and cultural relativism has instigated a sort of mental inflammation within the community of Iranian architects.

Abbas Riahi Fard, Kamran Heirati and Hooman Balazadeh, Ehsan Poud Textile Factory, Qom, 2007
The architects have here tried to capture a metaphoric interpretation of technical machinery and sewing machines in a textile factory.

Mahmoud Darvish, Polar Factory Mosque, Isfahan, 2003
Reuse of an improved traditional mosque typology with iwan entrances and main dome centrality.

conceptual patterns of Iranian architecture were employed with new interpretations. Entries by Mirmiran, Ali Akbar Saremi, Behrouz Ahmadi, Darab Diba, Iraj Kalantari and Hossein Sheikh Zeineddin, Farhad Ahmadi, Mohamad Reza Ghanei and Kambiz Navai among other well-known architects brought forth interesting potentialities and new outlooks.[10]

Defining the exact position of today's Iranian architecture elicits various points of view. The increasing importance of literature related to linguistic philosophy, Post-Constructivism, Structuralism, Deconstruction, semiotics, globalisation and cultural relativism has instigated a sort of mental inflammation within the community of Iranian architects. A pragmatism abstracted from the environment is one of the trends that has been developed in response to these stimuli, and is followed by some. However, despite discussions and literature that explain the 'Iranian-ness' of the projects, still many of the works are influenced by world architecture but without access to advanced construction technology.

If, during the Pahlavi era, Iranians regarded the achievements of Western civilisation as a model and pursued the imitation of Western designs, this was merely a feature of what then was regarded as progressive Iranian architecture. During the years following the revolution, in the struggle to achieve cultural identity, Iranian architects have turned towards revitalisation and fusion. The current trend emerging among architects such as Reza Daneshmir, Shahabeddin Arfaei, Hooman Balazadeh, Abbas Riahi Fard, Mohammad Majidi and Mahmoud Darvish is one accompanied by analysis, information and precise criticism.[11] They are taking strides towards recognising 'real' cultures, and they seek solutions in the opening of minds towards the world at large.[12]

Aware of a turning point in a global world in movement, parallel to spirituality, a dialectic discussion on causes and effects is emerging. By benefitting from global thinking, by acknowledging and incorporating the technological facilities of today together with inspiration from the universal abstract expression of Iranian architecture,[13] Iranian architects are trying to present, in the windows of pluralism and innovation, emerging paths for defining a new orientation.[14] The issue is no longer the search for cultural forms, but the understanding and intellectual awareness of what has always been the conceptual and philosophical essence of the artistic heritage of Iran.[15] ⌂

Notes
1. Nikki R Keddie and Rudi Matthee, 'Iran and the Surrounding World', *Interactions in Culture and Cultural Politics*, University of Washington Press (Seattle and London), 2002.
2. Homa Katouzian, *State and Society in Iran*, IB Tauris (London), 2006.
3. Yann Richard, *Entre l'Iran et l'Occident*, Editions MSH (Paris), 1989, pp 7–12.
4. Cyrus Ghani, *Iran and the Rise of Reza Shah: From Qajar Collapse to Pahlavi Power*, IB Tauris (London), 1998 and 2000.
5. Darab Diba, 'Iran and Contemporary Architecture', *Mimar 38: Architecture in Development*, March 1991, pp 20–36.
6. Nader Ardalan and Laleh Bakhtiar, *The Sense of Unity*, Chicago University Press (Chicago, IL), 1973.
7. Touraj Atabaki, *Iran in the 20th Century*, IB Tauris (London), 2009.
8. Jean-Pierre Digard, Bernard Hourcade and Yann Richard, *L'Iran au XXeSiècle*, Fayard (Paris), 2007, pp 154–87.
8. Darab Diba, the new Iranian national projects in *Contemporary Engineering and Architecture of Iran*, Ministry of Housing and Urban Development (Tehran), 1999.
10. Saeed Haghir, *Les Sources de l'Architecture Contemporaine en Iran*, Vols I and II, Editions universitaires européennes (Paris and Sarrebruck), 2010, pp 438–44.
11. Darab Diba, 'An Agenda for Architectural Journalism and Criticism in Iran', in Mohammad al-Asad (ed), *Architectural Criticism and Journalism: Global Perspectives*, AKTC (Geneva), 2006, pp 145–50.
12. Modjtaba Sadria, *Multiple Modernities in Muslim Societies*, AKAA (Geneva), 2009.
13. Darab Diba, 'A Life in Contemporary Iranian Architecture', *Architecture & Urbanism (Memari va Shahrsazi)* 100, January 2011, pp 27–31.
14. S Aliabadi, D Diba, KS Emami, S Katouzian, K Mehrabani and M Pourzargar, 'Paradoxical Tehran', *Domus* 901, March 2007, pp 46–50.
15. Michael Axworthy, *Iran, Empire of the Mind*, Penguin Books (London), 2007.

Text © 2012 John Wiley & Sons Ltd. Images: pp 70–1, 75(b) © Hossein Sheikh Zeineddin/Aga Khan Trust for Culture pp 72, 76–7 © Jassem Ghazbanpour; p 73(t) Courtesy of Shahbeddin Arfaei/Bam Citadel; p 73(b) © Nader Ardalan/Aga Khan Trust for Culture; p 74(tl) © Darab Diba; p 74(tr) © Farhad Ahmadi/Aga Khan Trust for Culture; p 74(b) Courtesy of Sharestan Architects and Planners/Behrouz Ahmadi; p 75(t) © Iraj Kalantari Taleghani; p 76–7; p 78(t) © Hooman Balazadeh/Aga Khan Trust for Culture; p 78(b) © Abbas Riahi Fard, Kamran Heirati and Hooman Balazadeh/Aga Khan Trust for Culture; p 79 © Mahmoud Darvish/Aga Khan Trust for Culture

Saman Sayar

Hadi Mirmiran, National Academies of the Islamic Republic of Iran, Tehran, 1994
Competition model illustrating how historical Iranian architectural elements such as the platform, dome and tower are assembled on site.

ASSIMILATING THE AUTHENTIC WITH THE CONTEMPORARY

THE WORK OF HADI MIRMIRAN 1945–2006

Hadi Mirmiran formulated a third way for Iranian architecture. During the 1980s he created an influential shift in thinking and practice by developing an alternative approach, which neither directly imitated Western Modernism nor copied traditional building forms. As **Saman Sayar** explains, Mirmiran developed a uniquely Iranian treatment that owed as much to the geometrical purity and simplicity of the 17th-century Bridge of 33 Arches in Isfahan as to Mies van der Rohe.

Hadi Mirmiran, Rafsanjan Sport Complex, Rafsanjan, Iran, 2002
above: The forms of the long, pure brick wall and brick dome resemble those of traditional ice houses.

I belong to a movement that aims to continue the evolution of architecture in this ancient land and to find its own place in the global context.
— Hadi Mirmiran, 1996[1]

Hadi Mirmiran was one of a new generation of Iranian architects who came to prominence at the end of the 1980s, after the eight years of stagnation caused by the Iran–Iraq war. Influenced by international architectural movements, he criticised Iran's modern architectural approaches, rejecting international Modernism as placeless and traditional Iranian architecture as outdated. Instead he sought to reconcile the two, linking contemporary design with Iran's rich heritage. To Mirmiran, the lessons of history and the slow evolution of form through time were being misunderstood and un-utilised. And whenever they were indeed utilised, it was done in a superficial manner. The contemporary modern movement has 'de-territorialised'[2] architecture with a self-imposed ignorance of historic achievement, and with that there has been a new desire to create architecture with

Mirmiran saw himself as concurrently part of a movement and part of a lineage of architectural achievement. The goal was not to reinvent architecture, but to improve upon the space history has presented us with.

reference to its time and place. Mirmiran saw himself as concurrently part of a movement and part of a lineage of architectural achievement. The goal was not to reinvent architecture, but to improve upon the space history has presented us with.

Mirmiran pursued these thoughts throughout his career, but particularly during his most productive time as managing director and principle architect of Naqsh-e-Jahan-Pars (NJP) consulting engineers (1989–2006). NJP worked on all kinds of projects, from small residential buildings, to embassies and regional and urban plans. Before founding NJP, Mirmiran was head of the design department in the main office of Housing and Urban Development of Isfahan province. From 1969 to 1979 he was the head of the department of Housing Design and Construction of the Iranian National Iron-Smelting Company. He received a masters degree in architecture with honours from the Department of Architecture of the Faculty of Fine Arts at Tehran University in 1968, and taught at the Elm-o-Sanat University Tehran, Iran-Azad University of Tehran, Hamadan and Shiraz. Throughout his career he received more than 25 architectural and urban planning awards including the First Degree Government Medal of Culture and Arts in 2004.

As discussed above, Mirmiran observed two general tendencies in Iran's contemporary architecture: one that follows international movements and one that follows traditional Iranian architecture. He concluded that these tendencies on their own were unable to create a compelling piece of contemporary architecture. Architects who had been following international movements, because of a lack of direct contact with the context or because of a time delay in transferring the principles, had mostly tried to imitate appearance with no mastery of the underlying concepts or ideas; while architects who followed traditional Iranian architecture mostly disregarded modern lifestyles and did not move beyond superficial imitation.[3] With this in mind, Mirmiran founded NJP with the aim of studying Iranian culture and integrating its concepts within the modern architectural movement.

In the schemes for the National Academies of the Islamic Republic of Iran (1994)[4] and the Rafsanjan Sport Complex (2002), one can clearly see Mirmiran's use of historical architectural forms, concepts and elements. In the National Academies of the Islamic Republic, historical Iranian architectural elements such as the platform, central courtyard and dome are composed gracefully. Consideration of the natural environment, an important aspect of traditional Iranian architecture, is evident in how the building conforms to its landscape, and in assuring views over Mount Damavand. Mirmiran was playful and confident with the use of these traditional elements, but translates them as a pure and modern aesthetic. Landscaping is introduced in a very light and contemporary way, as opposed to the more geometric treatment of landscaping in historic palaces.

There is similar geometric purity in the scheme for the Rafsanjan Sport Complex, a project spatially and structurally based on the traditional ice house, which comprises a cone-shaped dome and a long wall positioned so as to provide enough shadow and wind protection for a water pool where the ice is made. Similar to the spatial configuration of the ice house, the sports complex combines an opaque volume – the cone-shaped dome – with transparent elements, the wall and the

opposite: Interior view of the brick dome showing the concrete structure and the main stair.

above: Shading elements of the transparent glazed roof of the indoor swimming pool.

Hadi Mirmiran, Embassy of Iran in Bangkok, Bangkok, 2006
below: View of the garden from the central hall. The combination of water surrounded by trees is derived from traditional Iranian architecture.

right: Sketch of the longitudinal section and preliminary model illustrating the continuing line of water through the Embassy building.

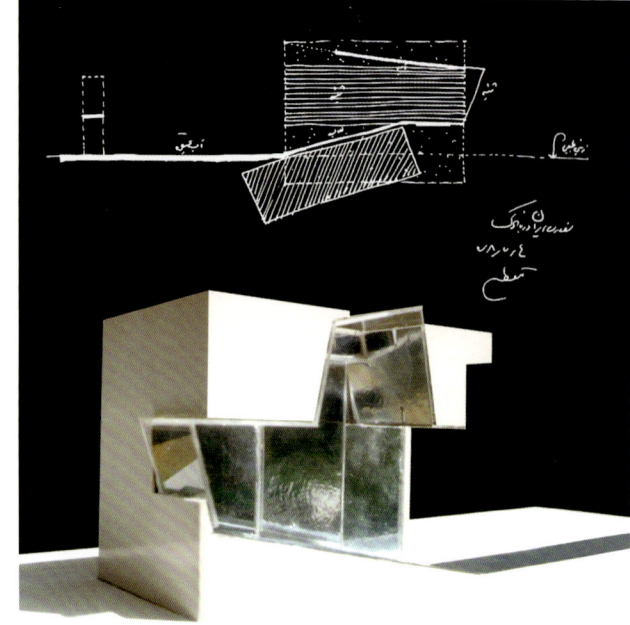

Mirmiran's design aesthetic developed from, on the one hand, the belief that architecture in different regions and periods is not isolated or individual, and on the other from a desire to tie his buildings to a certain cultural and historical background. All authentic architectural works have universal similarities.

right: The main building facade from the VIP entrance. The water line, mirrors and glazed surfaces evoke traditional elements of Iranian architecture, yet are placeless in terms of their application, arrangement and execution.

glazed roof, which expands over the covered and open-air pools, these being aligned in such a way as to form a vast surface of water. It is then divided by the transparent and diagonally latticed roof, which is intended to be reminiscent of ice. The external simplicity of the building is carried to the interior with its highly crisp and diverse divisions. Both of these projects evoke traditional forms but in a contemporary language, and are unmistakably regional.

Thus Mirmiran's design aesthetic developed from, on the one hand, the belief that architecture in different regions and periods is not isolated or individual, and on the other from a desire to tie his buildings to a certain cultural and historical background. All authentic architectural works have universal similarities. They follow both a process of theoretical and spatial creativity and a process of evolution that reduces material and maximises space. While there are essential similarities between the great works of architecture, all have evolved in a specific time and place, and that time and place has etched its mark on those works.[5] In the context of his projects, Mirmiran tried to create an architecture that was built with a universal aesthetic yet had a deep connection to traditional Iranian heritage. It was meant not only to reflect that heritage, but also to continue and advance it into the future.

These studies manifest themselves as metaphor and symbolism through minimalist design gestures. In the proposal for the National Library of Iran (1995), Mirmiran used the ancient contents of the 'protected golden tablet' as a symbol of knowledge. The concept of the project is the penetrating of the darkness of ignorance with the lightness of knowledge, and is driven by a classic Iranian poem about the power of knowledge: 'Watch the angel running after the devil, just as the melted gold runs once dripped over the tar.'[6] The idea of light and dark as a metaphor for ignorance and knowledge is common to many cultures, but this particular image of gold and tar is one that is particularly Iranian and is almost literally translated into a shiny, wavy black surface on which rests the golden object, the book repository. The two main programmes of closed book storage and reading areas are located on this dark surface. A glazed cover follows the shape of Damavand Mountain and contains these elements and spaces. This glazed transparent skin unifies the elements of the project and creates its form. Under this cover, several reading areas, lifted up into the space, are arranged along the main axis. The National Library exemplifies Mirmiran's use of symbolism and his references to Iranian culture and myth, and shows how he can translate these ideas and stories into architectural form.

Another major theme of Mirmiran's work and one that again originates from historical examples of Iranian architecture was that of transparency and lightness. In the Embassy of Iran in Bangkok (2006) he reduced the interior mass and integrated an outdoor garden by continuing a line of water through the building. This carries on through to the external skin, tearing it, and thus turning the interior space into a continuation of the exterior. It reminds one of the Iranian palaces and the gardens of the Safavid period (1501–1736), particularly the Hasht Behesht Palace in Isfahan. Material decreases as the interior

Hadi Mirmiran, National Library of Iran, Tehran, 1995
The glazed roof rises from the ground level creating a fifth facade for the building.

Mirmiran used the ancient contents of the 'protected golden tablet' as a symbol of knowledge. The concept of the project is the penetrating of the darkness of ignorance with the lightness of knowledge, and is driven by a classic Iranian poem about the power of knowledge: 'Watch the angel running after the devil, just as the melted gold runs once dripped over the tar.'

Concept model illustrating how the glazed roof unifies the various elements of the project.

Mirmiran understood space as a means of expression for an idea, and as such he sought to design not the space but the idea. If traditional architecture developed spaces with certain meanings, he wanted to use those precepts symbolically and not literally.

Hadi Mirmiran, General Consulate of Iran in Frankfurt, Frankfurt, 2004
View from the side of the building showing the rough volume suspended within a glazed case.

View of the multifunctional hall and glazed roof. The tree and line of water – elements borrowed from traditional Iranian architecture – create this transitional space between inside and outside.

expands and a floating transparent space replaces it. Much like in Hasht Behesht, the building is porous enough to be transparent, allowing the water feature and garden to approach the building via the main axis and to pass through it.

In the General Consulate of Iran in Frankfurt (2004), Mirmiran used a suspended mass covered in a glazed case. The rough lifted volume contains the private programme, and a transparent axis – the Gallery of Iran – connects the street and park through the building. This connection allows people to move about freely and to get acquainted with different aspects of Iranian history and culture, and functionally divides the project into two distinct parts. Daily bureaucratic activities are separated from formal diplomatic ones, which are covered with a semi-transparent glazed surface. The rough volume is raised on pilotis and provides a pleasant space on the ground floor for special ceremonies. Similar to traditional Iranian palaces and gardens, there is a fine and pure connection between interior and exterior space. A glazed space with trees and a broad, shallow band of water reflecting the elements of the building passes through the project.

Both embassy projects call upon the traditional garden to inform their formal and programmatic arrangement, demonstrating again that dramatic evocation of traditional elements can be achieved in a contemporary way. Even though Mirmiran's projects display a variety of forms, all have a very particular and similar process of design and development. He called this 'design's turning point, and elaborated that:

> For me, in the beginning of the design process the most important thing is finding the 'design's turning point' of the project. It means, knowing what the origin of the design is, and the main Idea of the project should be based on which factors ... the design's turning point in each project can be very different, sometimes it is a form, or a concept, a poem, or a memory, sometimes it is a dream, a myth, or an idea, and sometimes it is a combination of some of them, although I believe that the idea of a project should only be one, and even if it needs a combination of different ideas, we should always have a major one ... Eventually, the project's shape gets clear in your mind and at some point, you will have the final form and it's ready to develop by plans and models.[7]

Mirmiran argued that Modernism was developed at a certain time and a certain place and so it carries with it certain design gestures associated with that development. To transfer a movement that was essentially a reflection of the industrialised West wholesale to Iran would be wrong. Mirmiran was modern, but wanted to have a Modernism that was Iranian, that was developed in Iran, and that took into consideration all that came before it in that particular place. He considered Modernism a design process and did not feel the need to associate it with form. His designs created spaces with a minimum of lines, surfaces and volumes. Even when expressing the most sophisticated ideas he insisted on applying the most pure and simple forms and materials: a simplicity that was inspired by the purity of ancient Iranian architecture like Isfahan's Bridge of 33 Arches (*si-o-se pol*); the same simplicity in lines and surfaces that we see in modern Minimalist projects like Mies van der Rohe's Crown Hall (Chicago, 1956).

Mirmiran understood space as a means of expression for an idea, and as such he sought to design not the space but the idea. If traditional architecture developed spaces with certain meanings, he wanted to use those precepts symbolically and not literally. He designed his spaces to evoke the same principles of drama, transparency and lightness using the tools and techniques of the contemporary era. His work thus links the past with the present, and provides a template for the future, embracing history not as kitsch, but as a guiding source for a process that can create an authentic Iranian architecture: an architecture that is Iranian in spirit, but placeless and timeless in form. ᗭ

Notes
1. H Mirmiran, 'A New Movement in The Architectural Tradition of Iran', Lecture at the Architectural Association (AA), London, 24 January 1996.
2. Ibid.
3. Ibid.
4. Iran Urban Development and Revitalization Organization and Naqsh-e-Jahan-Pars (NJP) consulting engineers, *Mirmiran's Architecture*, Ministry of Housing and Urban Development (Iran), 1st edn, 2005.
5. Ibid.
6. Ibid.
7. H Mirmiran, 'Design Turning Point', *Architecture and Urbanism Magazine* 54(55), 1999, pp 62–4.

Final model. The transparent gallery divides the two main parts of the building.

Text © 2012 John Wiley & Sons Ltd. Images © Hamid Mirmiran, Naqsh-e-Jahan-Pars (NJP) consulting engineers

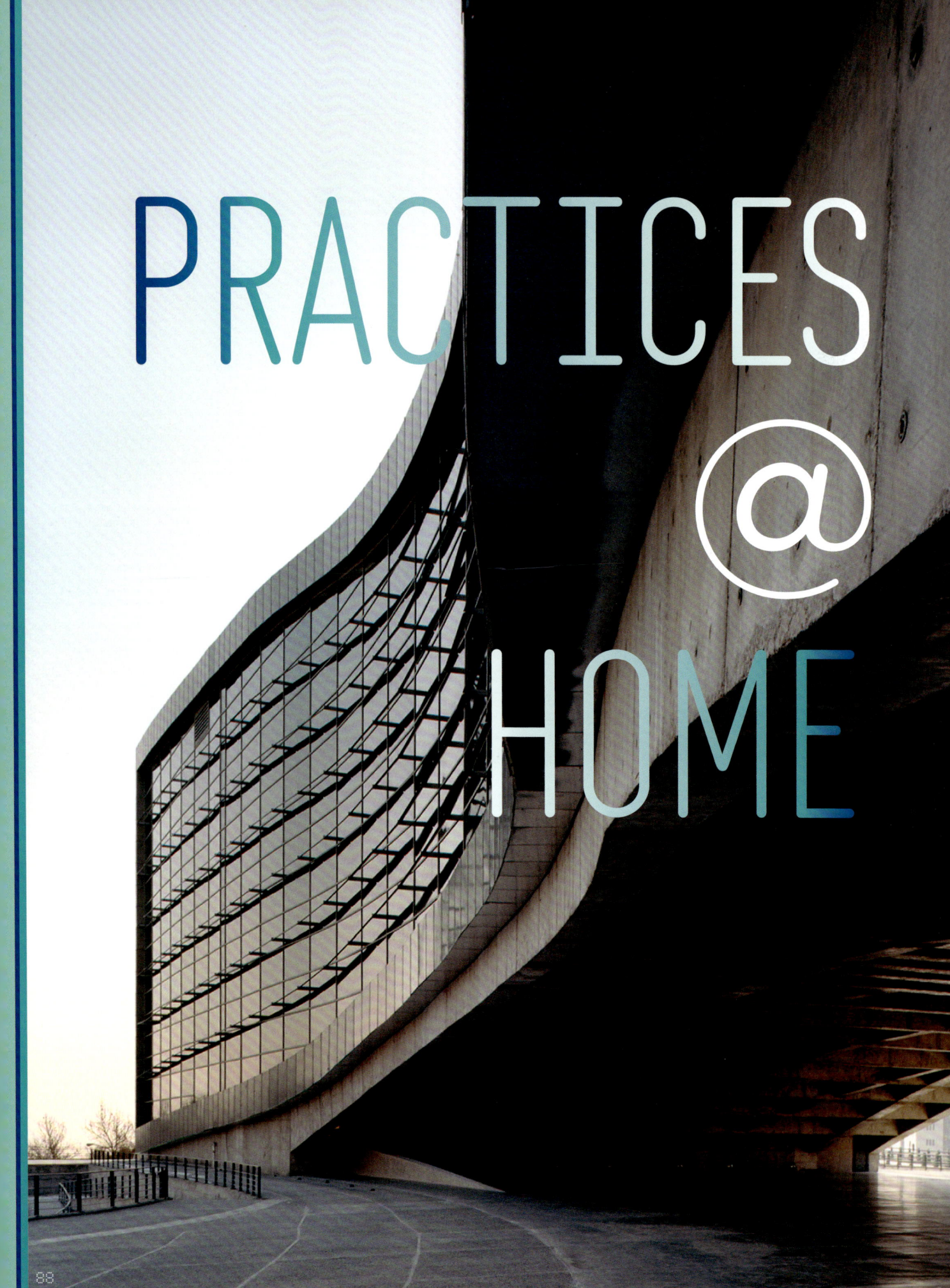

Mehran Gharleghi

ASSIMILATING THE PAST AND THE PRESENT FOR A VISIONARY ARCHITECTURE

Guest-Editor **Mehran Gharleghi** describes the work of four Iranian practices – Fluid Motion Architects (FMA), Pouya Khazaeli Parsa, Arsh Design Studio and Kourosh Rafiey/Asar Consultant Engineers' Co) – that are worthy

Over the last decade, architecture in Iran has witnessed a dramatic shift after a long period of confusion. This seems to suggest a transition from a situation where architects either uncritically followed Western movements or superficially replicated historical forms, to a period in which they are beginning to establish a generative feedback between their context and broader global movements. As Hadi Mirmiran argued in his lecture at the Architectural Association (AA) in London in 1996, great works of architecture across the globe and at different times share similar values.[1] This suggests the importance of understanding the global contribution of contemporary Iranian architects by way of examining their current work.

The current architectural discourse in Iran is rooted in the interaction between Iranian architects in Iran with those who studied and lived abroad. The dialogue and mutual influence between these groups set the foundation for the dynamic context of Iranian contemporary architecture. Bahram Shirdel, who returned to Iran in 1994, had a significant influence on Iranian architects, including Mirmiran, one of the most important leaders of Iranian contemporary architecture. While maintaining his core interest in traditional architecture, Mirmiran refined his work through collaboration with Shirdel from 1994 to 1996. In 1996 Mirmiran stated: 'I have been a practising architect for 27 years but only in a recent few years has my work been aligned with the views I express.'[2]

Thus Mirmiran went through a transition where broad reference to historical form, such as in the Rafsanjan Sport Complex (2002), was superseded by more subliminal use of the quality of the spaces in the traditional Iranian architecture, as in the Iranian consulates in Thailand and Frankfurt. The concurrent global and local developments catalysed the dialogue between the architects in Iran and the diaspora. The global recession and the reduced amount of opportunities in the West resulted in an increasing number of of international attention. Over the last decade, all have distinguished themselves by developing a body of work 'that is not only globally informed but also conscious and proud of its local, regional and national identity'.

Iranian diaspora returning back home. Some brought back with them the education they had received in various international schools of architecture. In the last two years, the presence of the AA Summer School in Iran, led by Omid Kamvari Moghadam, has helped a younger generation familiarise themselves with recent architectural developments and related software skills.

On the other hand, isolation and sanctions against Iran increased the urge to know about the outside world. Kamran Afshar Naderi, a professor at Azad University in Tehran and co-founder of the *Me'mar* journal, suggested that:

> *The cultural movement's driving force is the determination of Iran's most educated class to emerge from their shell to communicate with the outside world. For this reason, Iranians use any means available to help bring their message to the world. It is no coincidence that Persian is the fourth most-used language on the Internet.*[3]

This resulted in an architectural development that is not only globally informed but also conscious and proud of its local, regional and national identity. This is a unique movement worthy of international attention. It also raises concerns as to where this trend is leading. At this critical point in time, one needs to step back and evaluate the depth and qualities learnt from various cultures merged together to build our new environments. In this context the practices portrayed in this article – Fluid Motion Architects (FMA), Pouya Khazaeli Parsa, Arsh Design Studio and Kourosh Rafiey/Asar Consultant Engineers' Co) – have played an active role over the past decade.

Fluid Motion Architects (FMA)

FMA is an influential practice established by Catherine Spiridonoff and Reza Daneshmir. Daneshmir worked with Hadi Mirmiran from 1994 to 1995. He was invited back to the office as the project architect for a competition where he met Bahram Shirdel and worked for him for the next year and a half. He has been heavily involved with regional architectural discourse over the last decade and has served as a jury member for various competitions and awards.

The founding architects of FMA argue that their work attempts to integrate aesthetics, function and performance in line with the fundamental characteristics of traditional Iranian architecture. The Ave Gallery (Tehran, 2000) is one of their earliest constructed works and shows their interest in integrating form, function and aesthetics. Here, a disused swimming pool is transformed into an exhibition/gallery space. The main issue was the design of the enclosure and its connection to the gallery. However, the lateral split in the roof offered great potential such as defining the entrance area, lightening the structure, allowing light penetration to lower spaces, and vertical connectivity between the landscape outside and spaces inside.

Mellat Park Cineplex (Tehran, 2008) is FMA's largest constructed project so far and represents their focus on formal and spatial innovation, while being deeply connected to the surrounding urban context. The project won the Memar Award in 2008. It was designed and constructed on the far southwest side of Mellat Park, and its spatial organisation corresponds to the structure and programme, accommodating four cinema halls on an elongated site while allowing for interaction with the exquisite surrounding environment. Connecting the sloped faces of the two main cinema halls created a covered plaza (*eyvan*) that serves as a social interaction zone. In his 'Review of Contemporary Iranian and World Architecture', Iraj Etessam stated that the cineplex is the only valuable project in this area in 40 years and has completely changed the atmosphere and his feelings towards the park.[4] However, as Daneshmir suggests, a poor

Fluid Motion Architects (FMA), Ave Gallery, Tehran, 2000
top: Exterior view showing the simple yet dynamic roof geometry.

below left: A split in the roof accommodates the entrance to the gallery.

below: Interior view of the gallery showing the significant role of lighting and spatial organisation.

Their work attempts to integrate aesthetics, function and performance in line with the fundamental characteristics of traditional Iranian architecture.

infrastructural foundation and lack of parking spaces in the area results in limited public access to the project.

The success of the Mellat Park Cineplex was the incentive for the same client to commission FMA to design the Vali-Asr Mosque, also in Tehran and due for completion in 2013. The project is adjacent to one of the capital's most important landmarks: the City Theatre. Its surface creates an urban plaza that dissolves into the landscape as one gets closer to the City Theatre and then turns into a dome at the top. The roof opening allows for natural light penetration into the programme below. Despite their formal differences, the quality of the interior lighting and indirect organisation of the entrance resemble that of the Safavid period (1501–1736) Sheikh Lotf-o Allah Mosque in Isfahan.

Fluid Motion Architects (FMA), Mellat Park Cineplex, Tehran, 2008
top: The elongated footprint of the site made possible the creation of two long cinema halls at the lower level.

left: Vertical circulation and waiting areas benefit from natural light and views of the surrounding park.

below: A large covered plaza (*eyvan*) was created by placing the turning slope of the two cinema halls alongside one another.

Fluid Motion Architects (FMA), Mellat Park Cineplex, Tehran, 2008
below: With a total built area of 15,000 square metres (161,459 square feet), the project accommodates about 2,200 people during peak periods.

bottom: Diagrammatic section showing how the spatial organisation of the project correlates to the programme and structure.

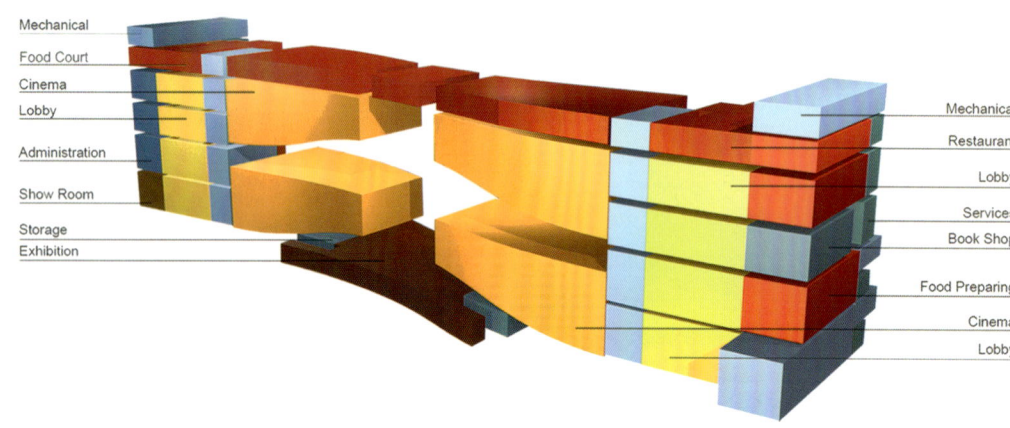

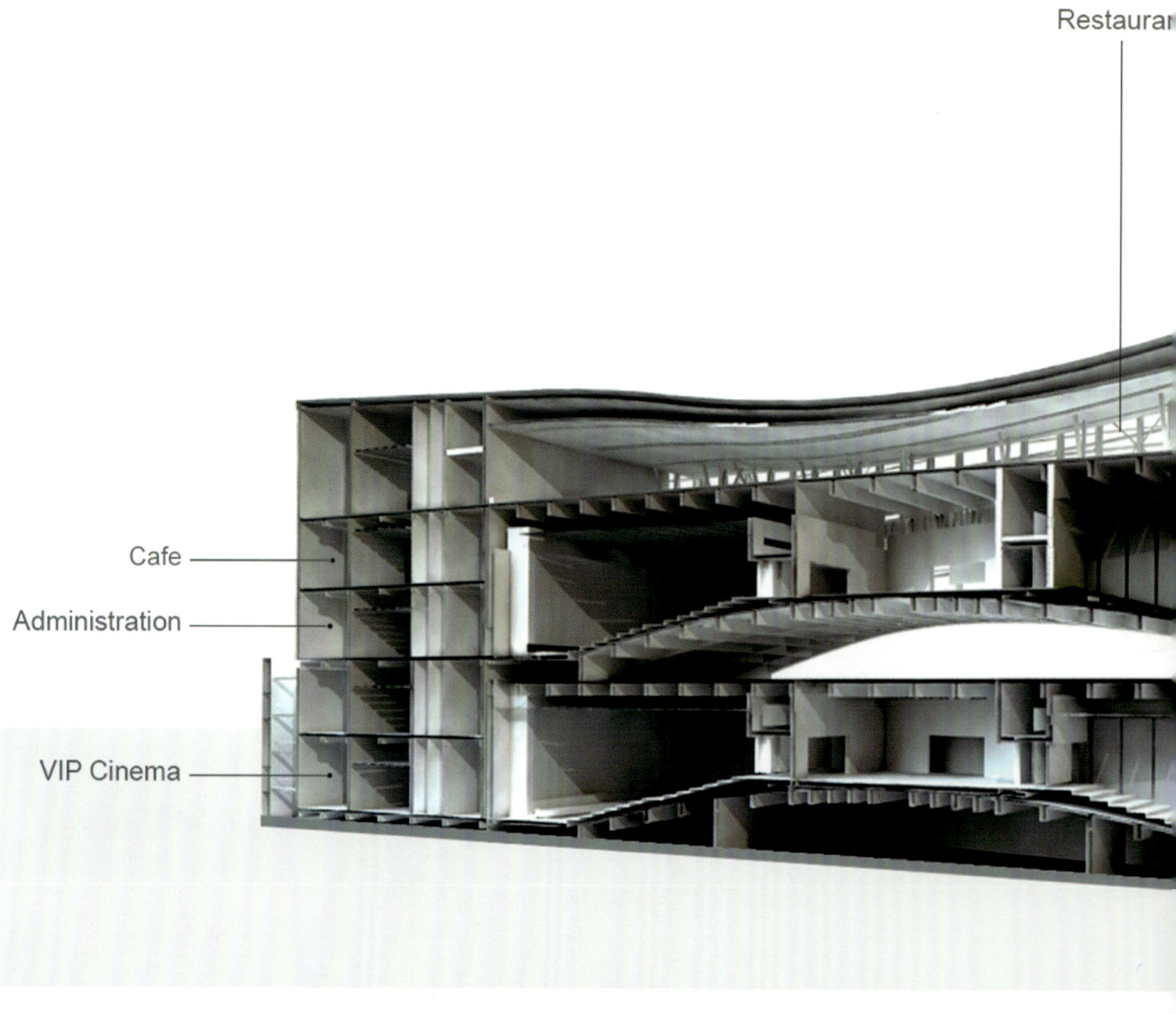

Fluid Motion Architects (FMA), Vali-Asr Mosque, Tehran, due for completion 2013
The mosque comprises a main undulating platform that dissolves into the surrounding landscape as it gets closer to the City Theater, providing public access to the plaza and preventing the theatre being blocked by adjacent buildings.

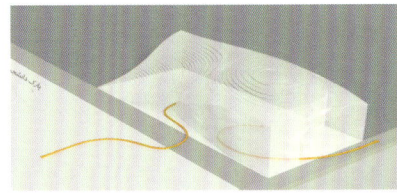

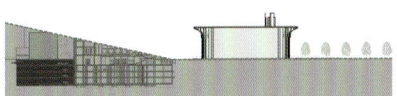

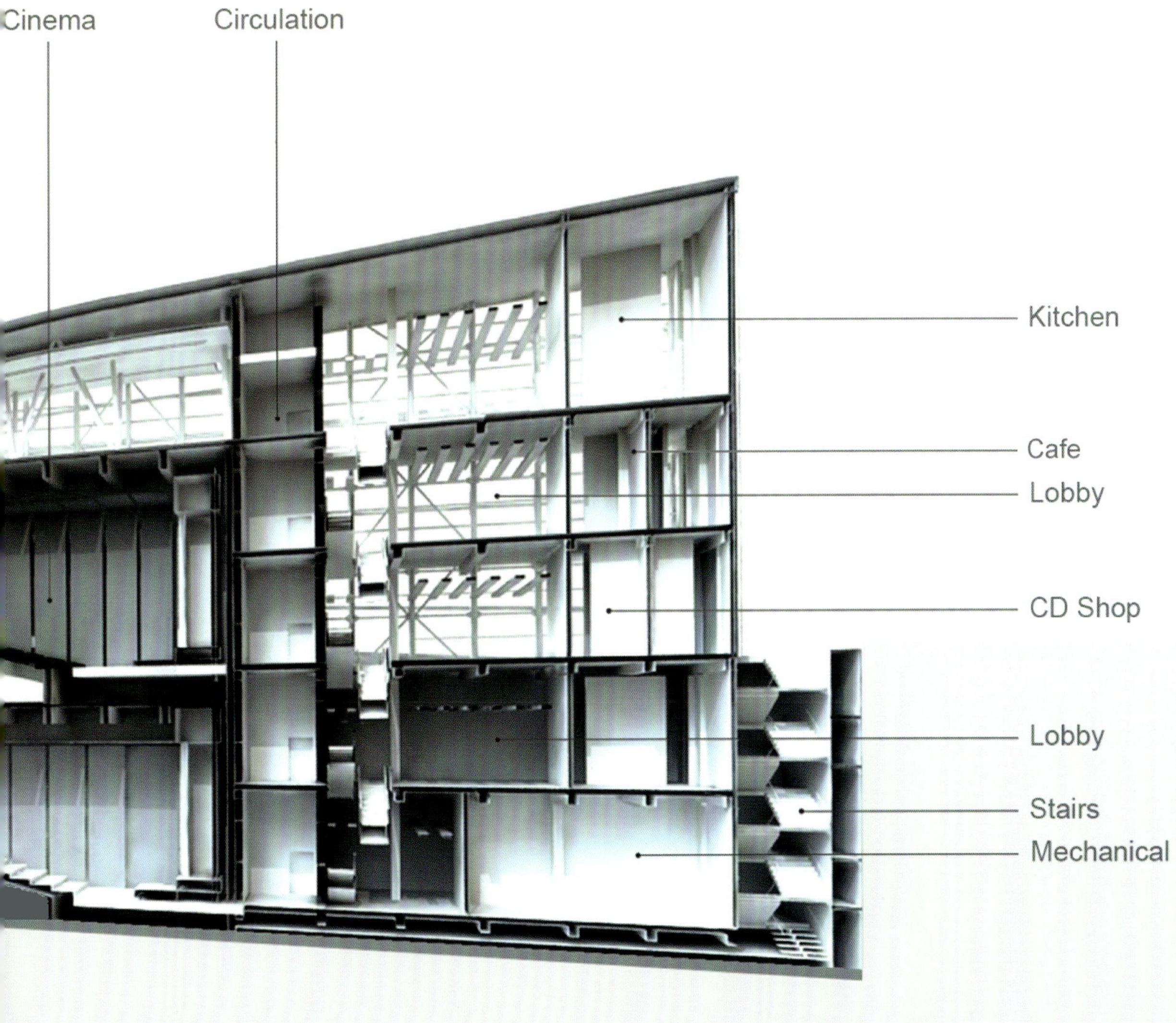

Kourosh Rafiey/Asar Consultant Engineers' Co

Kourosh Rafiey is a partner and the chief architect at Asar Consultant Engineers' Co. Ahmad Abrishami established the firm in 1980, and he currently holds the position of CEO. Rafiey has received prizes in numerous architectural competitions and served as a jury member in many competitions and awards. He believes the answer to each project lies within its own context or programme. By solving a project's specific questions, he attempts to achieve unique spatial qualities. This is most obvious in his 2009 Amaj Darman calibration laboratory project located in Pardis Technology Park, 20 kilometres (12 miles) from northeastern Tehran. The park provides a unique opportunity for a group of invited architects to construct iconic projects with high architectural value. The programme comprises a surgery room with affiliated spaces. The dynamic volume of the project is the result of a ramp extending from outside, which facilitates the distribution of the spaces within, including a laboratory, warehouse and all administration. The fluid movement of the ramp thus challenges the concept of interiority and exteriority. However, even though the geometrical consequence of the ramp movement within the building is appealing, what is missing is the quality of spaces that exist in kiosks (*kooshk*) within the Fin Garden in Kashan (1629) (see the article on 'Persian Gardens and Landscapes' on pp 38–51) and 'four-season' houses, a typology particular to the hot and dry regions of Iran where the interior and exterior boundaries are masterfully interleaved.

In 2007, Rafiey, in collaboration with Asar's Shervin Abrishami, was shortlisted in the competition for the Algeria Great Mosque & Cultural Centre. The design of the 'striated' architectural mass used in this project was first introduced to the Iranian context by Bahram Shirdel from his earlier works at the AA, and was adopted here as a means of spatially organising the Algeria Mosque. Lateral stripes are the central idea for the design of the massing and spaces. The project is inspired by the circular lines that pilgrims form around Mecca, which become increasingly dense as they get closer to Mecca and, eventually, around the Kaaba. These dense lateral stripes result in the dynamic interior space of the mosque.

Kourosh Rafiey, Amaj Darman calibration laboratory, Pardis Technology Park, Tehran, 2009
top left: First-floor plan.

top right: Second-floor plan.

bottom left: Interior view. The first and second floors house the laboratories and all administrative spaces. The floors are separated via a long ramp to provide an isolated space for the laboratories.

bottom right: The fluid movement of the ramp from outside to inside creates a smooth transition among various interior spaces and challenges the boundary between interior and exterior.

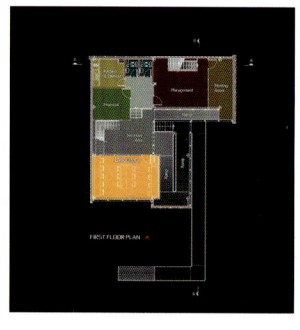
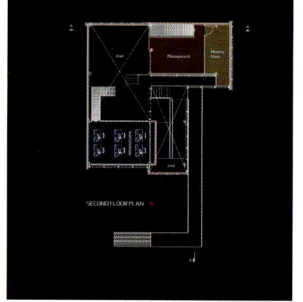

Asar Consultant Engineers' Co (Kourosh Rafiey and Shervin Abrishami), Algeria
Great Mosque & Cultural Centre, Algiers, Algeria, 2007

below and bottom: The parallel lines of the meridians were the inspiration for this proposal. Dense parallel stripes have been used to form a dynamic interior and a coherent overall geometry.

right: Internal spaces are generated from the movement of lateral stripes.

The project is inspired by the circular lines that pilgrims form around Mecca, which become increasingly denser as they get closer to Mecca and, eventually, around the Kaaba.

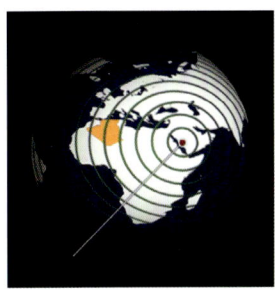
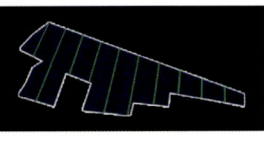
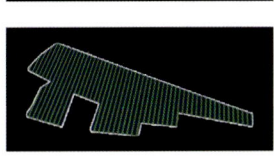

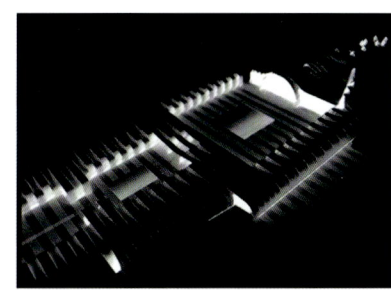

Pouya Khazaeli Parsa

Pouya Khazaeli Parsa is an architect and sculptor. He collaborated for a short period with Bahram Shirdel, from September 1999 to February 2000, with Hadi Mirmiran from March to September of 2002, and with Shigeru Ban from 2005 to 2007, and established Rai Studio in 2007. He has received numerous awards including first prize in the prestigious Memar Award 2009. His interest in spatial development through flattened, unfolded and axonometric drawings is rooted to Modern architecture, drawings and the paintings of Le Corbusier.[5]

It was this method he used in the design of Villa Darvish in Mazandaran, constructed in 2007, to articulate an ascending volume around a central courtyard and a raised living space. The use of narrow and elongated windows further references the project to that of the Modernist design. The dynamic volume rises to provide a view to the Caspian Sea that would otherwise be blocked by buildings in the vicinity. Rotation of the ascending geometry around a rectangle creates a central courtyard that is open from one side, generating a more private space yet allowing the wind to pass through the courtyard. In the humid conditions of Northern Iran, this significantly improves the comfort factor of the spaces that surround the central courtyard. The use of local materials, high spatial quality, response to the surrounding site and environment contribute to the quality of this project.

In 2009, it was in an experimental structure made from bamboo that Pouya Khazaeli excelled in the use of material and geometric logic; this was a project clearly influenced by his collaboration with Shigeru Ban. He went further in the Villa in Darvishabad (Mazandaran, 2010), shaping his own language by mixing the experience he had gained abroad with that gained in Iran. Here he created a transition from an enclosed space at the top to an open ground level. He organised the interior spaces around a central void, which takes its inspiration from traditional courtyard typologies. In this project a purely formal approach to traditional architecture has compromised the quality of the

Pouya Khazaeli Parsa, Villa Darvish, Mazandaran, 2007
below: The dynamic form of the building volume is a response to the views, surrounding site and the climate of Northern Iran. The central courtyard has been opened by raising one of the edges, allowing for natural cross-ventilation. This improves comfort in the extremely humid conditions and provides better views of the surroundings.

opposite left: Khazaeli Parsa's design method illustrated through flattened, unfolded and axonometric drawings.

interior spaces and the performance of the building. The arrangement of the rooms in the corners and placing the central void in the middle of the small living room reduce usable space. His method of using the principals of both Modern architecture and traditional Iranian architecture could be refined by further consideration of the proportions of his spaces, as Le Corbusier's Villa Stein (Garches, Paris, 1927) considers the proportions of Andrea Palladio's Villa Malcontenta (Mira, Venice, 1560).[6] On the roof garden Pouya Khazaeli created an open, yet private space by placing a high wall around the building boundary. The wall inhibits natural ventilation, creating an uncomfortable space in the humid environment of Northern Iran. In his earlier villa, natural ventilation was masterfully resolved while maintaining a private central courtyard.

Pouya Khazaeli Parsa, Villa in Darvishabad, Mazandaran, 2010
below: Interior spaces are organised around a central void similar to that of traditional central courtyard houses.

insert: The transition from an enclosed and private roof garden to an open-plan ground floor.

centre right: Pouya Khazaeli Parsa here began to develop his own interests, informed by his experience at home and abroad.

Pouya Khazaeli Parsa, Bamboo Structure, Mazandaran, 2009
bottom: Experimental structure using bamboo in an innovative way to synthesise material characteristics and fabrication logic and to accommodate the complex geometry. The choice of material is informed by the vernacular architecture of Northern Iran.

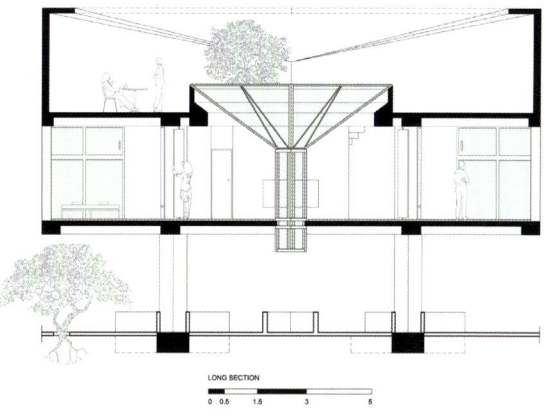

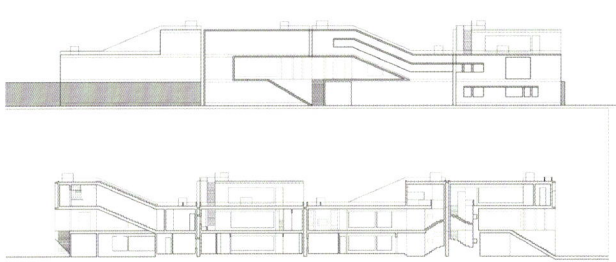

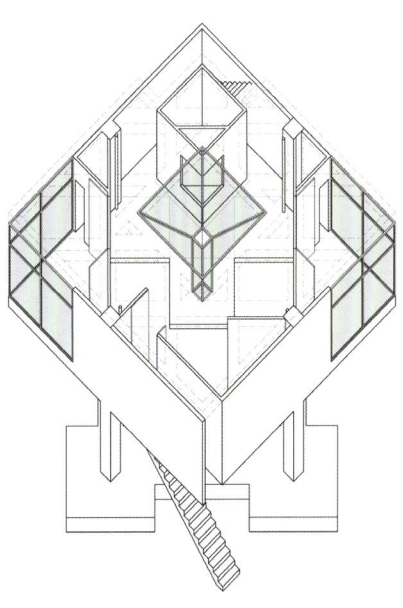

FIRST FLOOR -THE PRELIMINARY AXONOMETRIC

Arsh Design Studio

'[T]he desire for the shelter, privacy, comfort and independence a house can provide are familiar the world over.' From such a vantage point the characteristics of modern housing appear to transcend our own culture, being lifted to the status of universal and timeless requisites for decent living.

— Robin Evans, 'Figures, Doors, and Passages', 2009[7]

Arsh Design Studio was established in 2002. Rambod Eilkhani, Pantea Eslami, Nashid Nabian and Alireza Sherafati are the current partners and leading architects. Arsh has received various prestigious architectural awards.

The majority of Arsh's work is small-scale apartment buildings in Tehran. The urban density of the city arises from the vast amount of mid-rise, four- to five-storey apartment buildings. The exterior manifestations of such apartment buildings, in terms of the view from the street, are limited to single two-dimensional facades. However Arsh has attempted to raise the quality of the design and construction of these common building types from the two-dimensional facade into a more qualitative spatial design. The application of innovative construction techniques to affordable materials is a recurring theme in the firm's projects: Dollat I (2005), Dollat II and the Khorsand House (both 2007) and Office EEE (Enterprise, En Scène, Erratum) of 2010. Most of the housing projects benefit from a kinetic facade system that has a multiplicity of compositions based on the

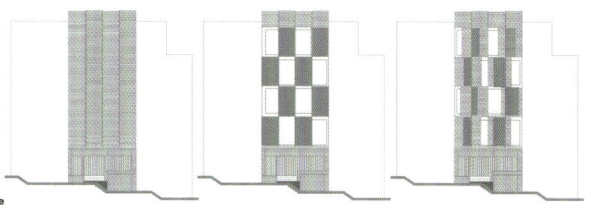

Arsh Design Studio, Dollat II and Khorsand House, Tehran, 2007
The adjustable wooden facades of these residential buildings generate a dynamic and ever-updating urban surface.

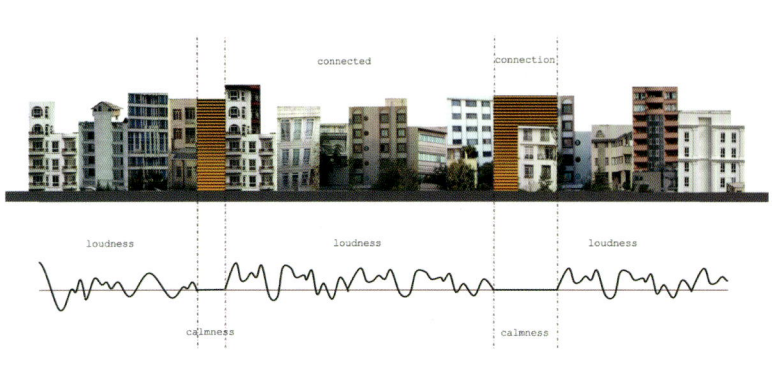

preferences and lifestyles of the inhabitants during various times of the day. Dollat II introduces a sectional variation into the conventional multi-stab section that allows for multiple unit types with varying square footage while providing access to the rooftop. Arsh's design strategy and use of material clearly varies based on the programme of the buildings. For example, Office EEE (Enterprise, En Scène, Erratum) was designed for two brothers, a geologist and a civil engineer, as their office space, and was built using exposed concrete. The exquisite detailing and finish of the building are not common in Iran's current construction environment. No wonder Arsh was shortlisted in the top 19 projects for the 2010 Aga Khan Award; its buildings suggest a dramatic shift in design and construction in dense urban contexts, a solution for shared concern across many cultures.

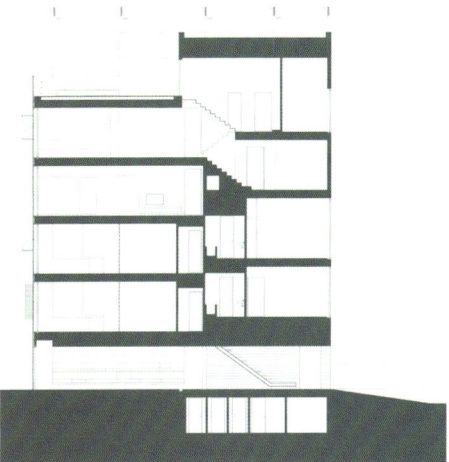

Arsh Design Studio, Dollat II, Tehran, 2007
A vertical shift to the conventional section enables a greater spatial diversity and access to the roof garden without compromising the constrained building footprint.

Arsh Design Studio, Office EEE (Enterprise, En Scène, Erratum), Tehran, 2010
below: The modest interior facade is a response to the surrounding residential neighbourhood.

below (top and bottom) and opposite: In Office EEE, Arsh Design Studio has paid extra attention to details and the innovative use of common construction materials.

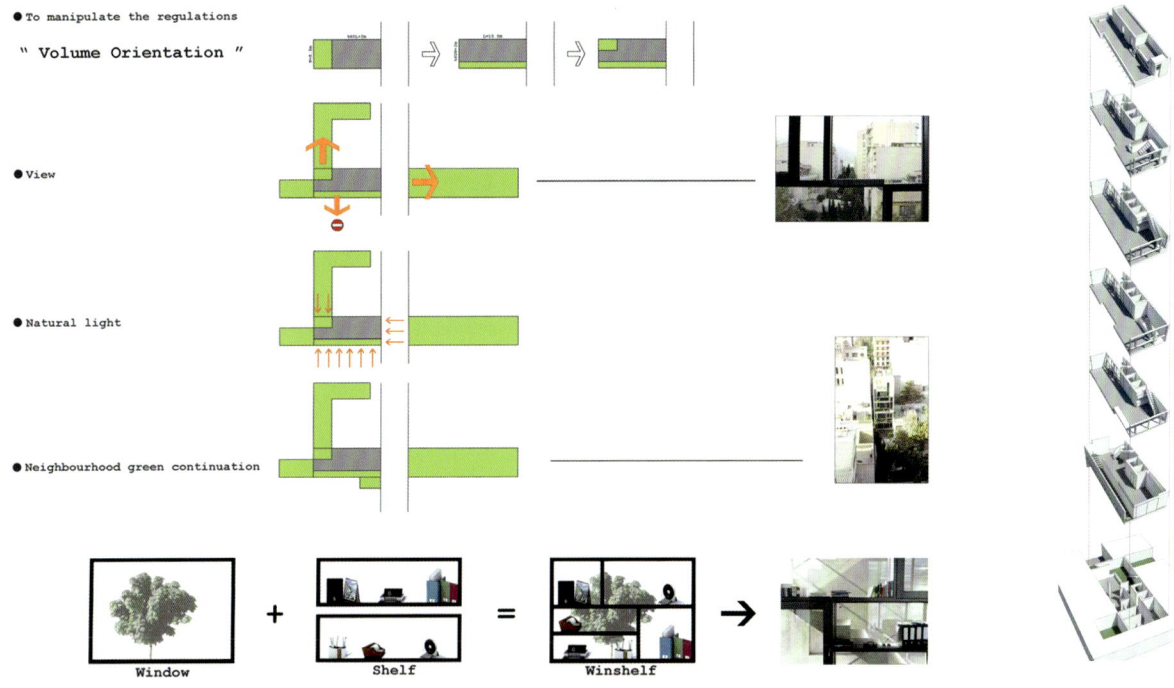

Looking to the Future

Recent developments in Iranian architecture are promising, in that they point towards an architecture that is the result of a reciprocal conversation between a 5,000-year-old culture and the opportunities presented by the world today. Millennia of cultural evolution have generated, throughout the various periods, architectures that have responded to cultural and climatic conditions and resulted in an immense degree of refinement and beauty. If current efforts will strive for a similar degree of refinement, a concerted discourse must be pursued that needs to stay clear of uncritical historical referencing while at the same time pursuing a detailed analysis of what makes particular projects of various historical periods interesting. It must also take into account the use of contemporary sensibilities, concepts, methods and skills, cultural patterns and processes, and local differences. It cannot be expected that high levels of integration of such considerations can arise from a relatively small number of projects in a relatively short period of time. However, in light of these realisations, this issue of $\varDelta$ can perhaps help to raise the stakes and fuel such a rich discourse that will require not only a strong effort among practices in Iran, but must also reach across borders while maintaining a cultural rooting. $\varDelta$

Notes
1. H Mirmiran, 'A New Movement in The Architectural Tradition of Iran', Lecture at the Architectural Association (AA), London, 24 January 1996.
2. Ibid.
3. K Afshar Naderi, 'Pouya Khazaeli Parsa, A Villa in Iran', 2011. See: www.domusweb.it/en/architecture/pouya-khazaeli-parsa-a-villa-in-iran/ (accessed 11 December 2011).
4. I Etesam, 'A Review of Contemporary Iranian and World Architecture', *Sharestan* 2(3), Spring 2010.
5. P Khazaeli Parsa, 'Corbu in Iran', *Domus906*, September 2007, pp 67–71.
6. C Rowe, *The Mathematics of the Ideal Villa and Other Essays*, 1st edn, MIT Press (Cambridge, MA), 1987.
7. R Evans, 'Figures, Doors, and Passages', in M Hensel, C Hight and A Menges (eds), *Space Reader: Heterogeneous Space in Architecture*, 1st edn, John Wiley & Sons (Chichester), 2009, pp 73–95. Evans quotes from DY Donnison, *The Government of Housing*, Penguin (Harmondsworth), 1967, p 17.

Text © 2012 John Wiley & Sons Ltd. Images: pp 88–9, 93 © Reza Daneshmir, photography Ali Daghigh; p 92 © Reza Daneshmir, photgraphy Ata Omidvar; pp 94–5 © Reza Daneshmir; pp 96–7 © Kourosh Rafiey; pp 98, 99(tr&bl) © Pouya Khazaeli Parsa; p 99(br) © Pouya Khazaeli Parsa, photo Mohsen Jazaveri; p 100–03 © Arsh Design Studio

Michael Hensel

PRACTICES ABROAD

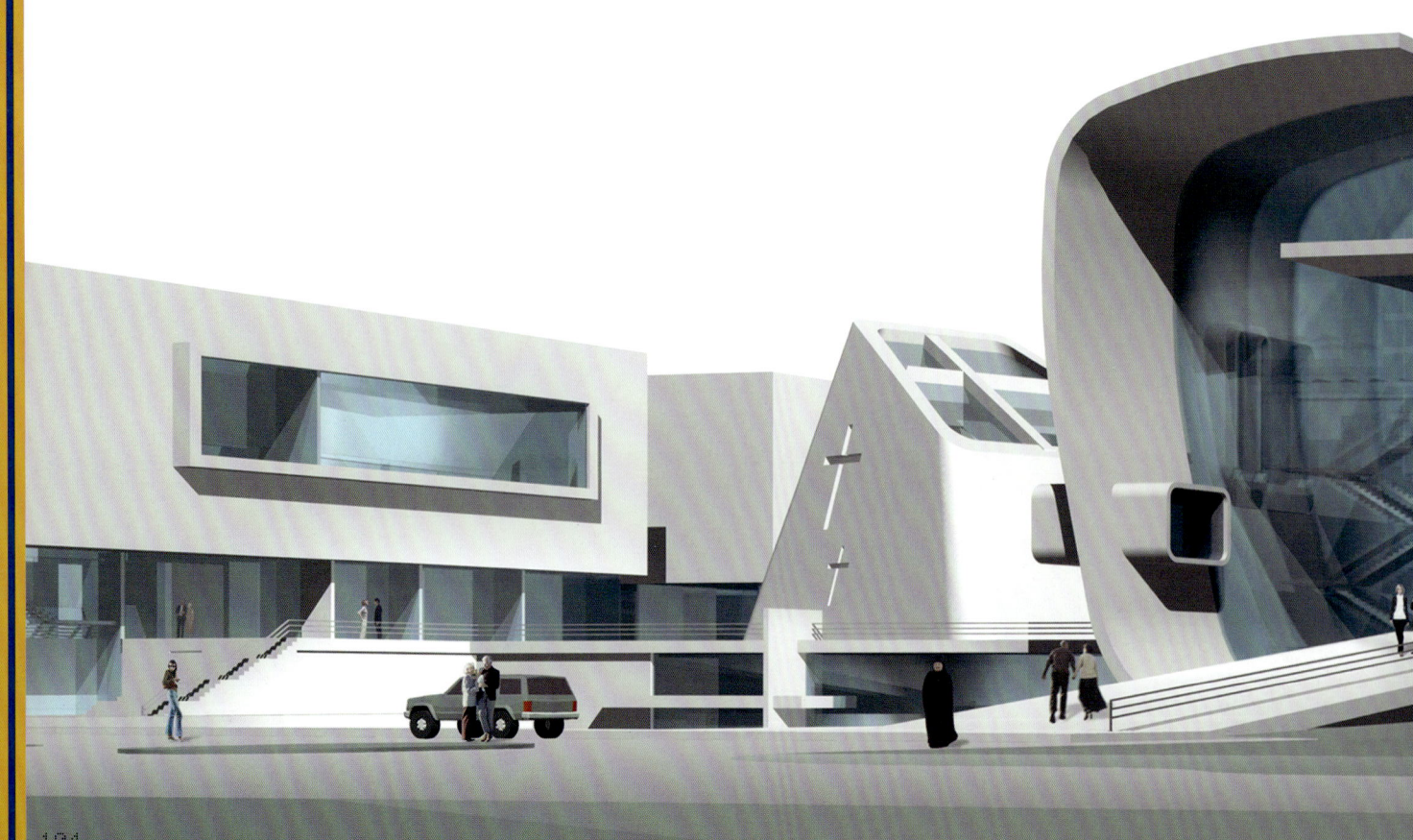

TODAY'S DIASPORA TOMORROW'S ARCHITECTURE

A surprising number of architects of Iranian origin, working outside of Iran, have come to international attention in recent years. Guest-Editor **Michael Hensel** looks at the work of US-based Hariri & Hariri and NADAAA, and

In recent years a significant number of architectural offices with principals of Iranian descent have come to prominence across the world. These include Farshid Moussavi Architects, Farjadi Architects and, most recently, Hariri & Hariri in New York, NADAAA (formerly Office dA) in Boston, Massachusetts, studio INTEGRATE in London, Atelier Seraji in Paris, and Yazdani Studio in Los Angeles. This development raises thought-provoking questions: Does a specifically Iranian sensibility underlie the works of these practices and, if so, what does it entail? Or do these architects have a general design sensibility that enables them to dominate more universal globalised series of approaches?

When squinting one's eyes it can perhaps be gleaned from the preceding articles in this issue that there are certain qualities that connect particular lineages of Iranian architecture, even though it is perhaps only by virtue of the prominence and teaching of specific distinguished Iranian architects. One of the most eminent Iranian-born figures is Mohsen Mostafavi, who was Chairman at the Architectural Association (AA) School of Architecture in London for over a decade and has since become influential in the US as Dean at Cornell and now Dean at the Harvard Graduate School of Design (GSD).

While this may or may not be true for architects who have at least been in part trained in Iran, it is not quite so obvious for those who

London-located Farjadi Architects and studio INTEGRATE. Chosen for the variety of their approaches, Hensel attempts to trace whether there are indeed shared connections and traits in their work that can be characterised as uniquely Iranian.

trained abroad, unless they were exposed to the teaching and work of distinguished Iranian architects who also lived abroad. The line becomes even more difficult to track as time goes on, with academics of Persian descent coming to the fore who were themselves born and educated abroad; for example, Nader Tehrani, who is now Professor and Head of the Department of Architecture at the Massachusetts Institute of Technology (MIT), was born in England and educated at Rhode Island School of Design and at Harvard.

Some of the Iranian practices located abroad are led by Iranian architects, while others combine partners of different nationalities. Until its recent break-up in June 2011, London-based Foreign Office Architects (FOA), with the Iranian–Spanish partnership of Farshid Moussavi and Alejandro Zaera-Polo, was one of the most distinguished examples of the latter.

The four practices featured here, Hariri & Hariri, NADAAA, Farjadi Architects and studio INTEGRATE have been chosen for the apparent differences in their approaches to work to examine whether, despite these variances, there are some connections indicative of the common traits of Iranian architecture, and to try to trace actual and latent potentials inherent in their respective works.

Hariri & Hariri

In 1986, sisters Gisue and Mojgan Hariri founded the practice Hariri & Hariri in New York City. The office undertakes projects on a wide range of scales from product design to small buildings, as well as large-scale buildings and urban ensembles. What is striking at first glance is the difference in design approach relative to the various scales. At the object scale, two different design languages coexist: a more playful Modernist one, and another that is more freeform and material effect related, as can be seen in the firm's designs for the Rock Crystal Chandelier (2006), Crystalline Bath Collection (2008–11) and the Liquid Chaise (2007), which seem to celebrate the sensibility of architectural effects at the product design scale. In private residences, a more disciplined Modernist language prevails. Projects such as the Wilton Pool House in Connecticut (2007), the Sagaponac House in Long Island (2004) and Belmont House in California (2002) give ample evidence of this and feature varying materials and textures. The large-scale buildings return to a more playful Modernist language. This includes projects such as The Cine in Brooklyn (due for completion in 2020) and the Rockland Center for the Arts in West Nyack, New York (2010). The urban ensembles combine a more reserved Modernist language with a more playful one for key buildings, such that projects like St Mark's Coptic Canadian Village (Toronto, 2003) could be a well-designed part of Chandigarh. What seems to be a recurrent theme is the wrapping surface that defines the designs of, for example, the Wilton Pool House, as well as the larger-scale schemes such as the Business Bay Dubai Tower (2007–), which seems to resemble a reuse of the firm's design for the Museum for the 21st Century in New York. At any rate the larger-scale and unbuilt projects are almost invariably shown in computer renderings as white in colour and smooth in texture. Their material articulation is thus quite varied across scales. And so one begins to wonder what would happen if the commitment to the production of formal and material effects that features in some

Hariri & Hariri, Wilton Pool House, Wilton, Connecticut, 2007
The design of the pool house features a sculptural surface that appears to warp around the interior and provides covered exterior space.

Hariri & Hariri, Pyramids of Spiritual Harmony, St Marks Coptic Canadian Village, Toronto, 2003
below and pp 106–7: The scheme takes on a Corbusian formal language, combining a series of more normative perimeter buildings with the sculptural language of the cathedral characterised by a wrapping surface, a recurrent theme in Hariri & Hariri's work.

At any rate the larger-scale and unbuilt projects are almost invariably shown in computer renderings as white in colour and smooth in texture. Their material articulation is thus quite varied across scales.

of Hariri & Hariri's best designs at the product scale would meet the surface sensibilities of their building-scale projects? Is there a hidden Iranian sensibility that occasionally shows through? At this present moment this question will remain unanswered. However, one can begin to imagine how, for example, the Rock Crystal Chandelier would inform the larger-scale projects with a nuanced formal and material sensibility that is culturally and context specific. It might seem that the scheme for the Business Bay Dubai Tower is beginning to move in this direction.

Hariri & Hariri, Liquid Chaise, 2007
Some of the furniture designed by Hariri & Hariri begins to acquire a more fluid, organic formal language.

Hariri & Hariri, Rock Crystal Chandelier, 2006 and Crystalline Bath Collection, 2008–11
These Swarovski crystal products are characterised by a faceted freeform design.

Hariri & Hariri, Business Bay Dubai Tower, Dubai, 2007–
In this high-rise scheme, the theme of the wrapping surface reoccurs, but here as a type of screenwall that makes reference to those of the Islamic world.

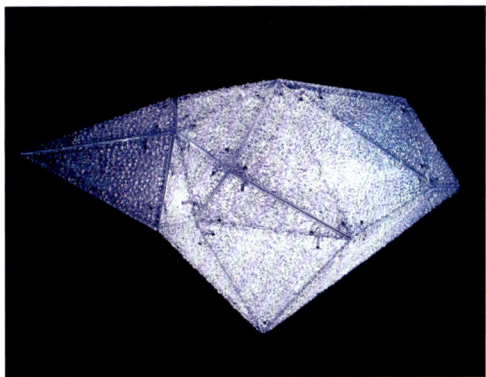

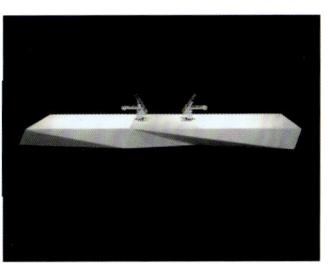
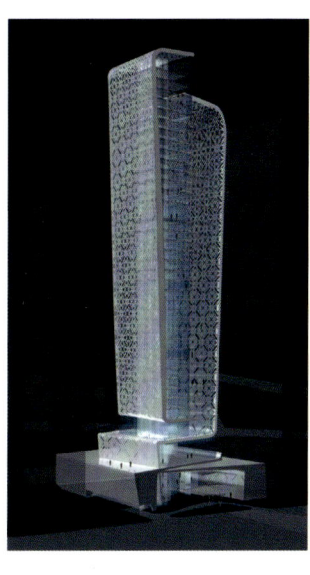

109

Farjadi Architects

In 1989, sisters Homa and Sima Farjadi founded Farjadi Architects in London. The practice has designed projects for a great variety of geographical and cultural contexts that are often characterised by an explicit landscape approach to specific aspects of each. This frequently includes the organically articulated footprint and volume of the architectures. Moreover, there exists the recurrent theme of a landscaped surface, and space on the ground floor and concourse areas of the projects in section, such as in the schemes for the Quimin Research Library and Museum in Yunan, China (2011) or the Suzhou Park Development (Jiangsu, 2011), or alternatively one that wraps the building, such as in the Linzhou Tourist Information Centre (Henan, 2011).

Farjadi Architects undertook these recent schemes in collaboration with Turenscape China. The projects undoubtedly benefit from their landscape context and accentuate this quality by translating it into a corresponding tectonic, suggesting new possibilities for architectures that might arise from a landscape urbanism approach. It will therefore be interesting to see how this design approach will be both maintained and modified in an urban context. What is equally noteworthy is the design of the building envelopes, such as the one that undergoes gradual transitions from opaque to transparent by way of varying the diamond-shaped cladding in the Quimin Research Library scheme. Something similar seems to be intended with the varying density of vertical tubular elements that make up the envelope of one of the main buildings in the Suzhou Park Development. However, it seems that these schemes do not entirely wish to negate and dissolve the object a la Kengo Kuma.[1] Instead they suspend the object in a state between alternating dissolution and accentuation. Where will this approach go from here, and how might the landscape approach to the ground level and the concourse areas leave the Modernist constraint behind and transform the whole into a more intense and expansively landscaped sectional scheme?

Farjadi Architects and Turenscape China, Suzhou Park Development, Jiangsu, China, 2011
This scheme for a redevelopment an old cement factory adjacent to a canal features an intensified land- and waterscape, and the design of a new building that partially constitutes a constructed landscape.

Farjadi Architects and Turenscape China, Linzhou Tourist Information Centre, Henan, China, 2011
left and right: The masterplan for the tourist information centre features a building design characterised by a wrapping surface that creates a constructed landscape set within an intensified land- and waterscape.

Farjadi Architects and Turenscape China, Quimin Research Library and Museum, Yunan, China, 2011
below and bottom: Here, a building mass floats above a constructed landscape, emphasising and extending the hilltop location.

NADAAA (formerly Office dA)

Launched in January 2011, NADAAA can be regarded as a new manifestation of Office dA, which Nader Tehrani co-partnered for 20 years with Venezuelan architect Monica Ponce de Leon. At NADAAA, Tehrani directs the office together with his partners Dan Gallagher, previously Vice President of Office dA, and Katherine Faulkner, who brings with her 20 years of detailed design and management experience from outside the practice.

NADAAA/Office dA works across a wide range of scales, including products, furniture, installations, small- to large-scale buildings and urban design. Its work is marked by a decidedly non-standard approach that is most restrained and rigorous when standard elements like brick are used, such as in the Tongxian Art Center (2001) and Tongxian Gatehouse (2003) just outside Beijing. Semi-finished products such as sheet material in material assemblies are often tamed by the base geometry of the elements that are subsequently varied to enable freeform designs. This approach is apparent in the 2006 Helios House 'green' gas station in Los Angeles that NADAAA/Office dA collaborated on with Johnston Marklee and Big, or the Banq restaurant in Boston, Massachusetts (2008).

Where it gets really interesting is when functional requirements are imposed to develop freeform architectures. In the example of the Helios House Gas Station, various renewable energy and rainwater-related requirements were considered. While the former had no real impact on the freeform design, the rainwater was to be collected and conducted to a corner of the site to sustain a water garden. Here, form and function enter into an integral relationship. However, If the various building elements would be intensively multifunctional, the geometric sensibility would be put to thought-provoking task both in its overall and detailed articulation. The loop back to the integral formal–functional sophistication of past Iranian architectures could easily be instigated, as the geometric and material rigour

NADAAA/Office dA, Banq, Boston, Massachusetts, 2008
left: Exploded axonometric of the different tectonic elements of the scheme that evokes a cavernous image or one of a carved space.

right: Interior views.

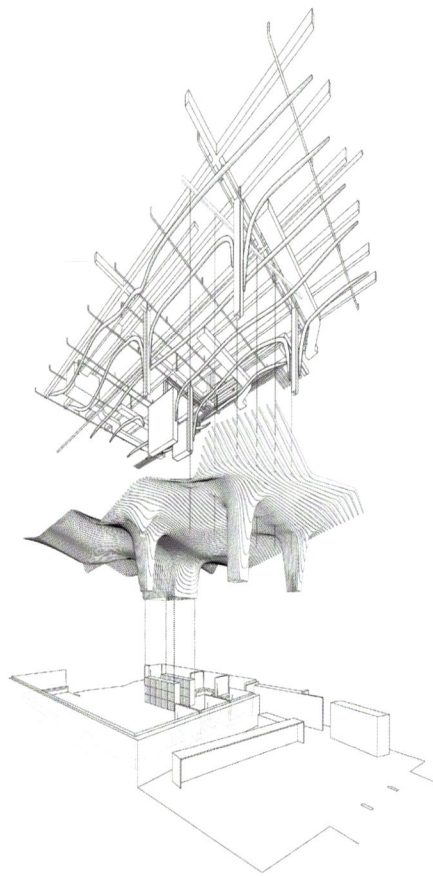

is already present. On a corner site in LA, it is not so entirely clear how context could assert itself more to inform the design. This type of consideration could, though, inform the production of microclimate as an additional provision not unlike that in some of the projects analysed in 'Towards an Architectural History of Performance' on pp 26–37. For this to be possible, the more general contemporary trend towards differentiated geometry, material system variation, non-standard architecture and so on would need to be put to task in an increasingly specific manner. How would NADAAA's work veer in this direction?

NADAAA/Office dA, Tongxian Gatehouse, Beijing, 2003
The variation of the brick surface delivers a rich texture to the building volume.

NADAAA/Office dA with Johnston Marklee and Big, Helios House Gas Station, Los Angeles, 2007
top: Artificial lighting of the triangulated surface during the dark hours of the day evokes the double image of a cavern with stalactites and a distorted Islamic vault.

above: The expressive sculptural character of the gas station is in stark contrast to its nondescript urban context.

below: The collection of rainwater on the roof of the expressive design and through permeable pavers is used for irrigating the vegetation including a small water garden.

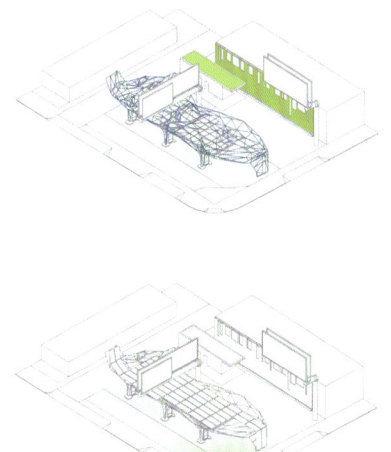

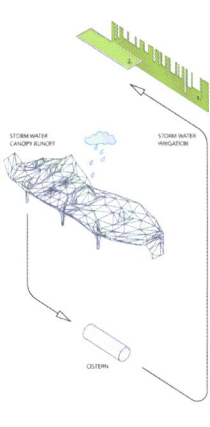

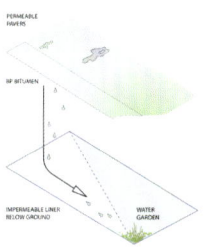

studio INTEGRATE

In 2009, Mehran Gharleghi and Amin Sadeghy launched London-based studio INTEGRATE. The two architects studied first at Tehran University of Science and Technology, and afterwards at the AA in London. Moreover, they worked with distinguished architects in both locations, including Dr Nasrine Faghih and Hadi Mirmiran, and for a short time Bahram Shirdel in Tehran and Foster + Partners and Plasma Studio in London. As a result of this, they combine a pronounced personal interest in and knowledge of the cultural context of Iran with the global outlook of London. In their work they take up traits of historical Iranian architecture, such as Islamic geometry and the performative capacities of historical Persian architectures, and combine these with contemporary concepts, design concerns and analytical methods. The influence of the approaches of Mirmiran, Faghih, Shirdel and Foster is clearly present in their work, but markedly transformed through their interest in the sophistication of the past and the technological affordances and potentials of the present, as well as the new complexities arising out of the combination of these.

The studio's projects are all marked by this distinctive amalgam and they seem to have no qualms about continuing to collaborate with their former teachers on design and research projects. This is indeed refreshing in a general context in which those that strive for innovation believe or pretend that they can, or already have, singlehandedly reinvented architecture. Clearly studio INTEGRATE seem to think in the long term and carefully direct their own development with open eyes and minds.

Their most accomplished projects to date are their proposals for the World Carpet Trade Center in Tabriz (2007) and Benetton Headquarters in Tehran (2009), and the commissioned Saba Naft project (studio INTEGRATE with Nasrine Faghih and Archen Consultancy) in Tehran (2010). Although all three projects are quite different in appearance, they are at the same time marked by a similar set of concerns: the integration of geometric

studio INTEGRATE and Nasrine Faghih, World Carpet Center, Tabriz, Iran, 2007
The proposal develops an Islamic ornament into a building envelope that provides a heterogeneous interior environment. The main volume of the building floats above a sizeable ramped surface that connects the urban surface to the interior, suggesting an enormous urban carpet that acquires three-dimensionality.

below: development of the envelope pattern.

bottom: Axonometric view.

top: Night views.

complexity, spatial organisation, material effect and environmental conditioning. Ultimately this amounts to a concern regarding the quality of provisions for human inhabitation. This is what inherently characterises these projects, and one should not be sidetracked by the apparent similarities to other contemporary projects of seemingly similar geometric expression. While studio INTEGRATE's work celebrates the role of geometry, it never descends into mere exuberance for the fun of it, nor have any of the historical projects that are so dear to Gharleghi and Sadeghy. Thus far they have managed to stay on the straight and narrow. Furthermore, they aim to synthesise their experiments and research into pneumatics systems and their environmental modulation capacity into their large-scale work.

Large parts of the Saba Naft facade are articulated by such a pneumatic system. Heavy materials are used to frame space while the light pneumatic systems are used to condition it. In the Benetton and World Carpet Trade Center projects, a similar approach is present, only materialised in a different manner. What remains somewhat unresolved is both a more intense internal and external spatial agenda. For example, Shirdel's earlier work constitutes a particular challenge to standard building sections, as can be seen in the Nara Convention Centre (Nara, Japan, 1993), which utilises a box-in-a-box section.[2] It seems odd that non-standard architecture should stop short of unfolding its full potential by leaving the standard column and slab arrangement of normative architectural sections intact. It would seem that the whole effort invested in the envelope should yield conditions that would assert themselves against the standard section and associated plan arrangements, if one considers, for example, the sophistication of the sectional organisation of Ostad Ali Maryam Kashani's 19th-century Boroujerdi's House in Kashan (see page 36).

studio INTEGRATE and Nasrine Faghih, Benetton Headquarters, Tehran, 2009
The articulation of the building volume in this proposal suggests an image of the dissection of geological mass by a tight canyon with a crystalline surface, or an Islamic vault violently distorted by the rotational movement of a cyclone. The geometrically highly articulated inner surface and the veiling outer one generate a heterogeneous field of material effects, while the tight 'courtyard' space enables passive environmental modulation.

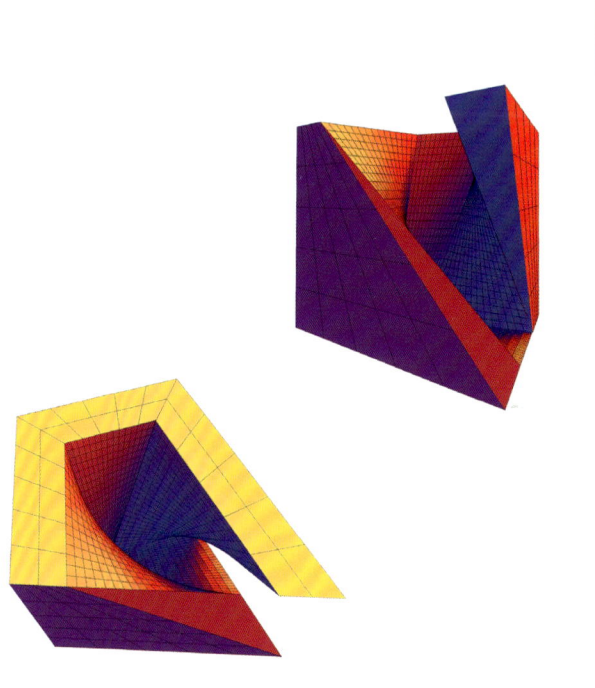

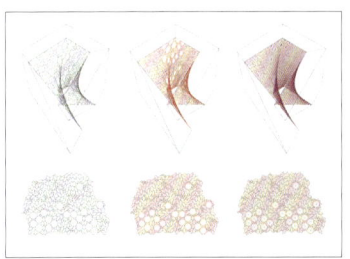

studio INTEGRATE with Nasrine Faghih and Archen Consultancy, Saba Naft, Tehran, 2010
Like the Benetton scheme, this project features two distinct parts of the building envelope: a more straight-lined opaque and framing one, and a curvilinear and geometrically highly articulated one. However, while the Benetton scheme is more introverted, Saba Naft is explicitly extrovert, using its massing to orient the interior towards or away from climatic influences.

top, bottom and opposite top: Environmental analysis and design strategies.

opposite bottom: rendered view.

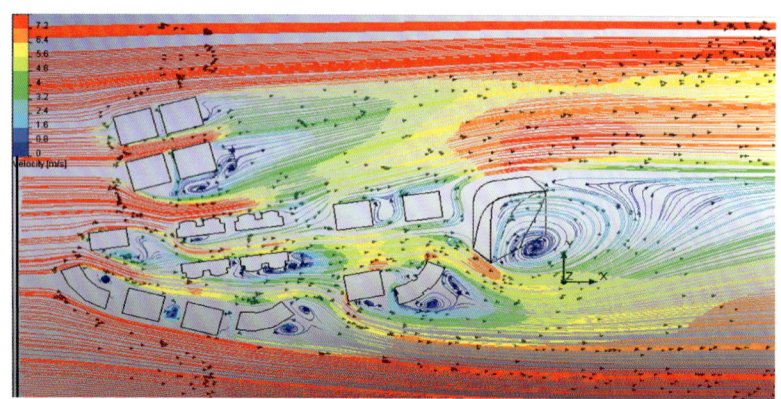

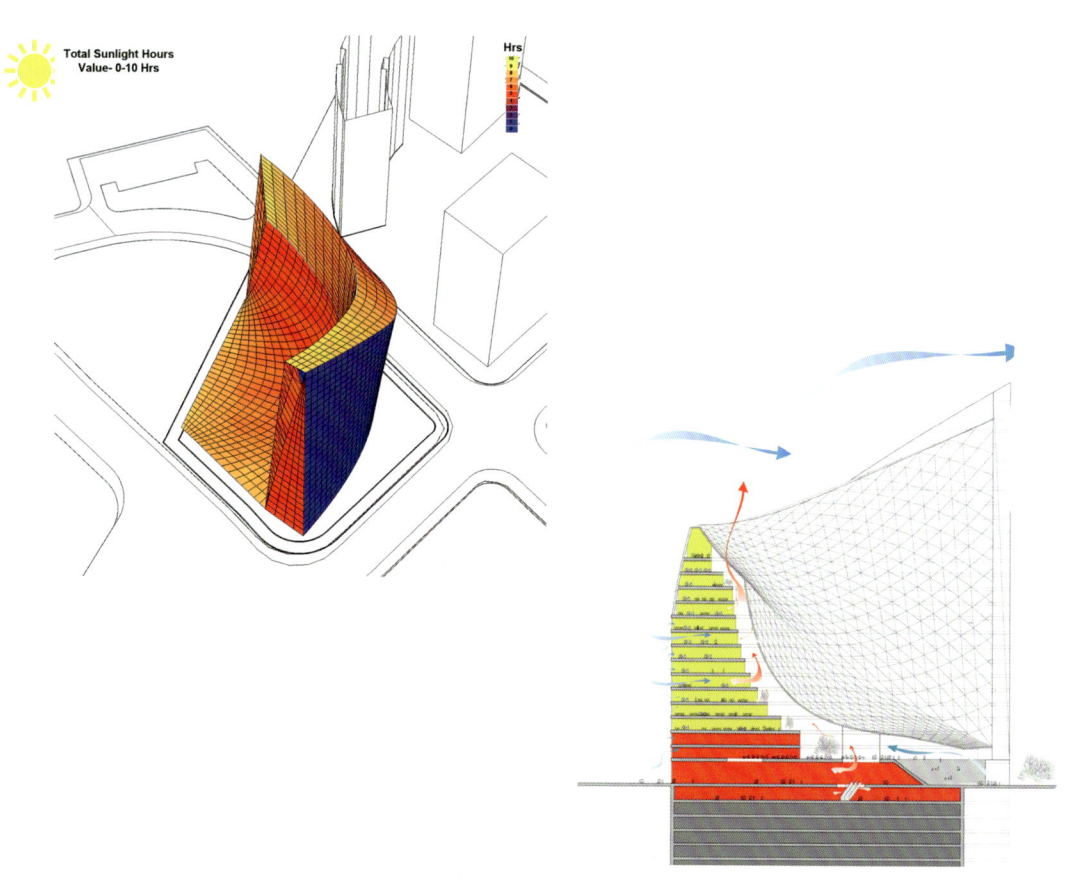

116

Viewing platform
Offices
Hypermarket
Open platform
Parking

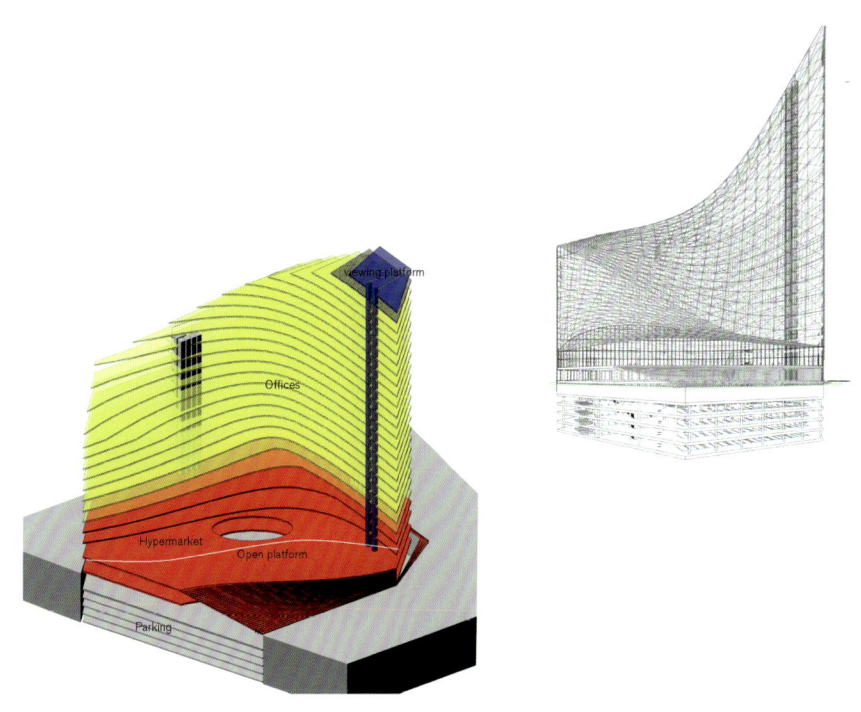

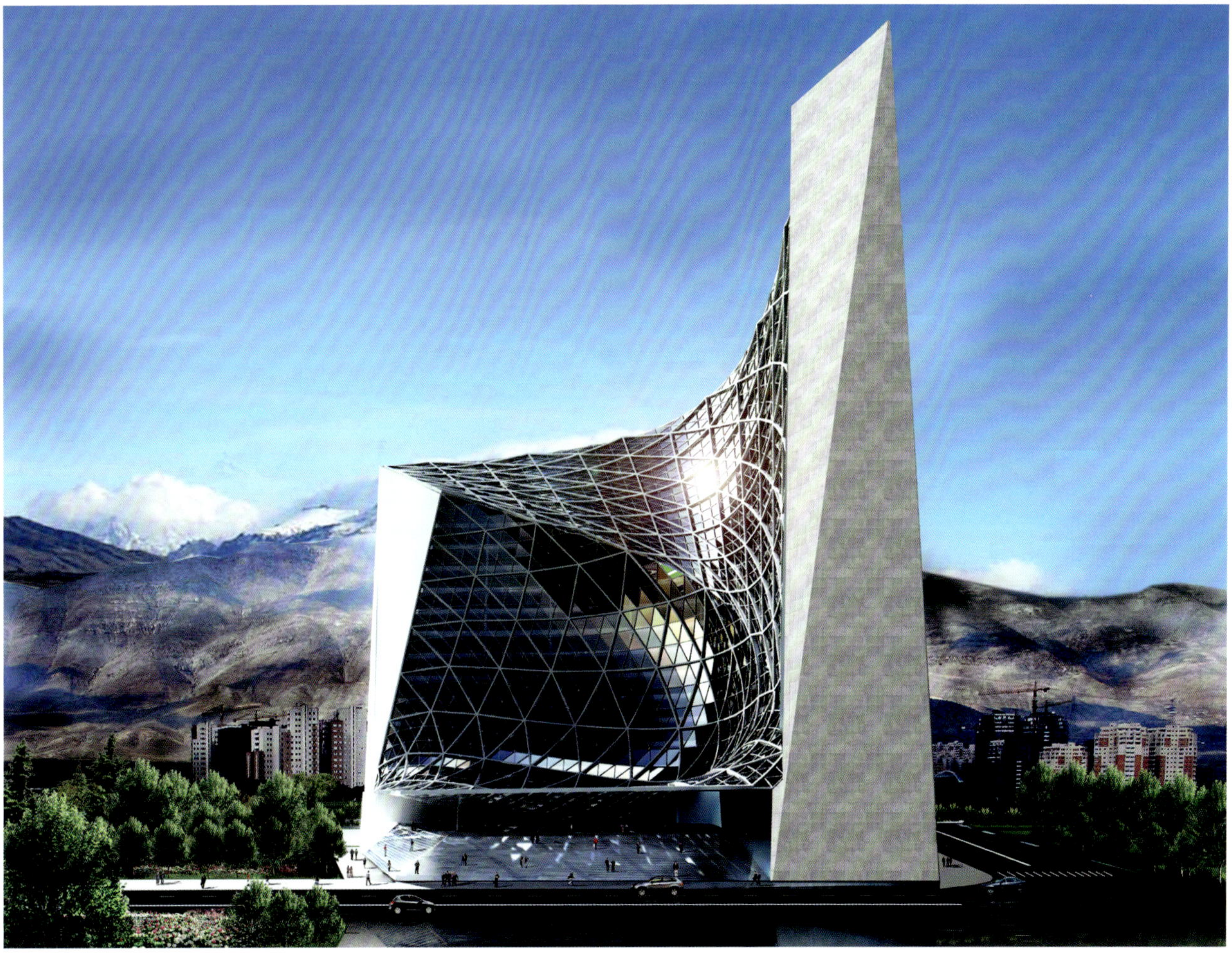

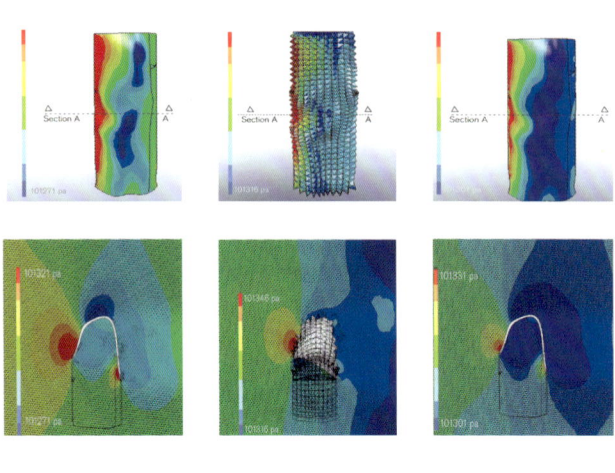

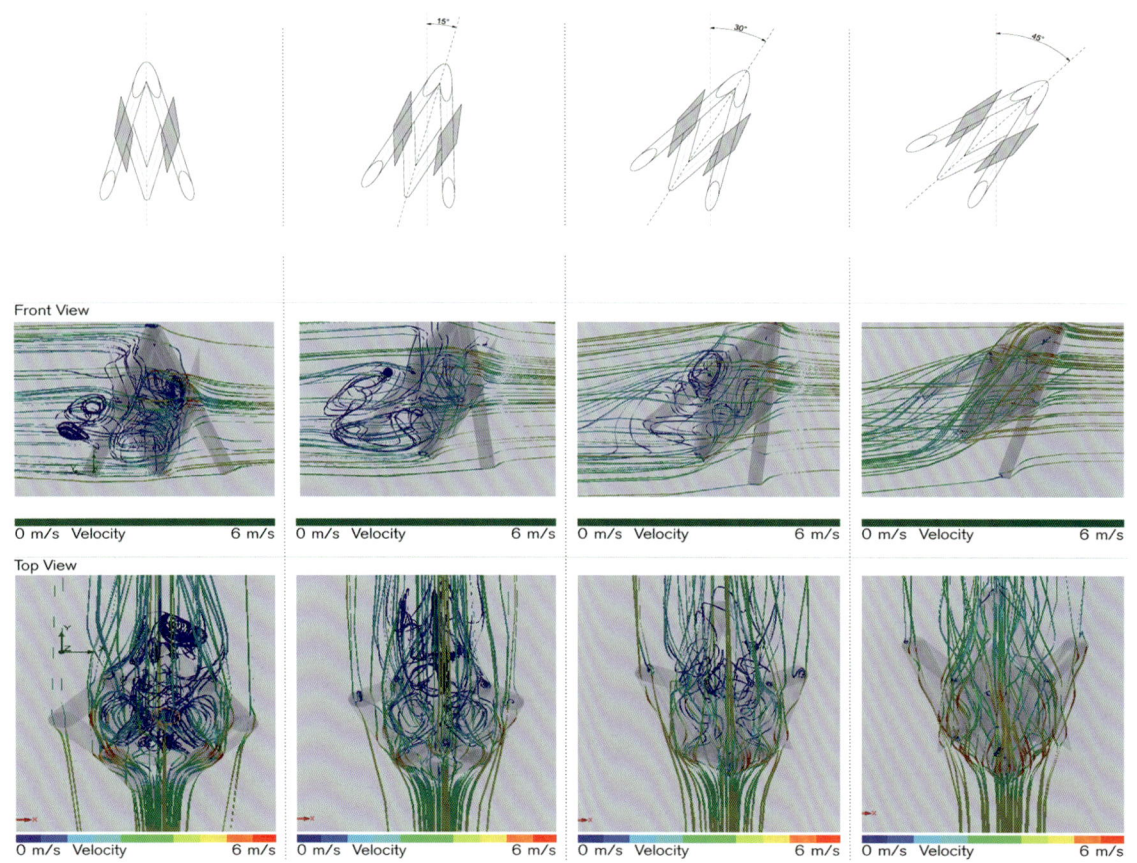

studio INTEGRATE, Adaptive Pneumatic System Research, 2008–
Research into differentiated pneumatic systems and their use in climatic modulation has been a recurrent theme in the work of studio INTEGRATE. Whether full-scale prototypes or schemes like the Saba Naft facade, their command of this particular material system is promising.

opposite top left and bottom: Differentiated assembly of environmentally responsive pneumatic elements.

opposite top right and right: Computer fluid dynamic (CFD) analysis of the airflow across and through the assembly.

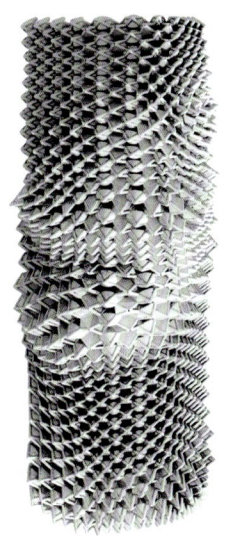

Looking Forward

How might the designs of the different practices here be informed by an increasingly specific consideration of context above and beyond what constitutes current practice, either a fabulous landscape or other great architectures? The point, however, is not to promote large-scale parametric urbanism designed by the respective offices as the total exterior project, but instead to see how, and in many aspects, particularly well-designed buildings meet a context of similar such buildings designed by others, no matter from which period in time. This would help to overcome one of the most unhelpful entrenched dialectics of our time: space and place.

To conclude, it remains difficult to say whether architecture produced by Iranian practices abroad shares traits in an evident enough manner to posit a clear contemporary Iranian architecture. What is clear is that certain current themes and inclinations prevail that are shared by other practices across the world. However, in a time that is at once generally eclectic and globally streamlined in terms of architectural design, there are particular aspects and qualities present in the designs of Iranian practices abroad that are entirely worth nourishing and developing in highly specific ways. To do this may require looking both forwards and backwards, and employing a culturally specific analytical mindset. We may then perhaps begin to see what may characterise Iranian architectures in their full refinement in different parts of the world. ⌂

Text © 2012 John Wiley & Sons Ltd. Images: pp 104–5 © Hariri & Hariri Architecture; pp 108(t), 109(t&br) © Hariri & Hariri Architecture; p 108(b) © Hariri & Hariri Architecture, photo Paul Warchol; p 109(c) © Hariri & Hariri Architecture, photo courtesy Swarovski Crystal Palace; p 109(bl) © Hariri & Hariri Architecture, photo Karin Kohlberg; pp 110–11 © Homa Farjadi – Turenscape; pp 112(l), 113(b) © NADAAA/Office dA; p 112(r) © NADAAA/Office dA, photos John Horner; p 113(t) © NADAAA/Office dA, photos Eric Staudenmaier; pp 114–19 © studio INTEGRATE

Notes
1. K Kuma, *Anti-Object: The Dissolution and Disintegration of Architecture*, AA Publications (London), 2008.
2. J Kipnis, 'Towards a New Architecture', ⌂ *Folding in Architecture* 63(3–4), 1993, pp 40–49.

Michael Hensel

LATENT FUTURES OF IRANIAN ARCHITECTURE

How is it possible to draw on inherited technical and cultural knowledge while being projective and anticipating an evolving future? **Michael Hensel** highlights the value of recognising essential Iranian sensibilities and identifying salient past traits that can be redeveloped into an enlightened contemporary approach. What sort of novel amalgamations might point towards the most promising futures for Iranian architectural design?

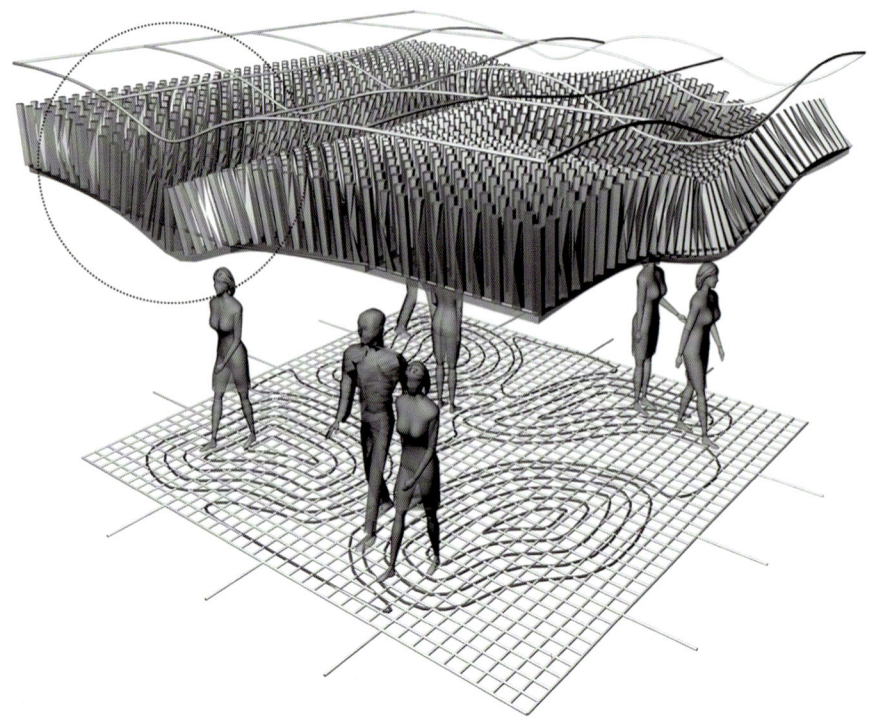

Michael Hensel, Potential Futures of Iranian Architectures, 2012
Past and numerous present Iranian architectures display key traits of what might be called 'performance-oriented architecture'. They engage local climate, material performance, an active architectural boundary, articulated envelopes, extended thresholds between exterior and interior, auxiliary relations to extensive human-made or natural systems, and related evolving settlement pattern and processes. Contemporary examples of Iranian architectures engage the ground in promising ways, but could learn more from the auxiliarity traits and the settlement pattern and processes of the past, as well as engage more intensively with the local geo-ecological context. If future Iranian architectures succeed in integrating the accomplishments of past and present ones, there will be a lot to look forward to.

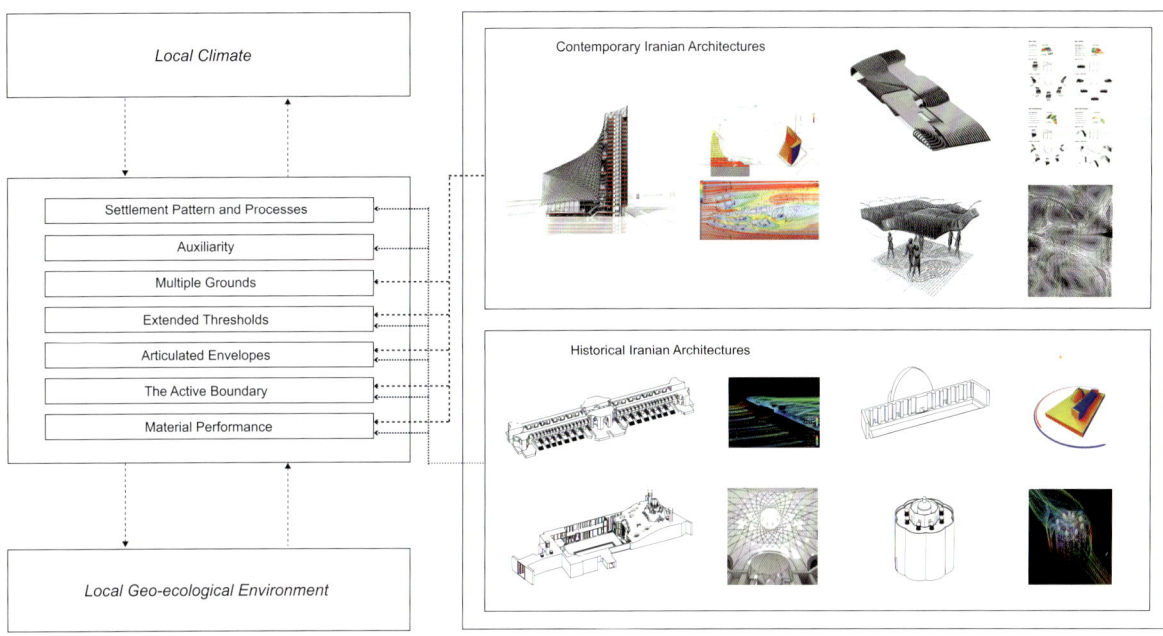

If architectures are to be relevant and projective, architectural discourse will need to lead the way. To attain these qualities across anything but a very limited spectrum of work, discourse must be analytical and reflective; it must draw concurrently from significant past and present achievements and, furnished with related insights, perceive promising futures. At best such dialogue links realised, latent and novel potentials into new permutations.

Current dominant 'discourses' tend to focus on universal themes of architecture or on highly specialised ones from which, so it is frequently hoped, the former will arise. Rarely, however, do these currently address the potentials of locally specific sensibilities and associated aspects of context-specificity that have evolved over time, and their continued and conceivably increasing importance in the context of so-called globalisation and the complexity of sustainability.

Too tempting is the attraction of veering towards the idiosyncratic and the wish of the architect or critic to stand out, style-conscious clients and patrons permitting. In the stead of substantial discourse this has insistently bred superficial monologues that are presented with relentless sanguinity. This striving for idiosyncrasy comes habitually hand in hand with an unenlightened stance that rejects calls for overarching and integrated discourses as academic, and criticality as negativism. Such posturing merely satisfies the self-interest of those who consider themselves prodigious.

Nevertheless, the problem at hand and the associated need for rethinking have frequently been addressed throughout previous decades. In 1964, for example, Christopher Alexander pointed out what continues to be a contemporary problem:

> Bewildered the form-maker stands alone. He has to make clearly conceived forms without the possibility of trial and error over time. He has to be encouraged now to think his task through from the beginning, and to 'create' form he is concerned with, for what once took many generations of gradual development is now attempted by a single individual ... The intuitive resolution of contemporary design problems lies beyond a single individual's integrative grasp.[1]

Related to the disconnection of contemporary design from gradual developments over time is the difficulty that Kenneth Frampton addressed in his formulation of a critical regionalism in 1983. Frampton outlined the problem by quoting Paul Ricoeur: 'How to become modern and to return to the sources; how to retrieve an old dormant civilisation and take part in universal civilisation.'[2] However, as Frampton pointed out, it is essential to avoid 'simple-minded attempts to revive the hypothetical forms of a lost vernacular'.[3] In 1986, Hassan Fathy offered a promising way forward:

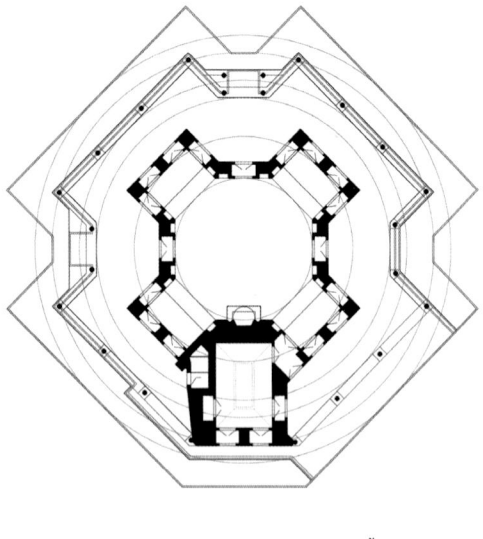

Michael Hensel, Fin Garden Kiosk, Kashan, Iran, 1629 and Baghdad kiosk, Topkapi Palace, Istanbul, Turkey, 1638–9
left, below and all opposite: These two kiosks display two very different types of spatial organisation. The Fin Garden kiosk (opposite top and right) features its most enclosed spaces in plan on the four corners and is transected along its two central axes by exterior space. The Baghdad kiosk (left and bottom left) features its most enclosed space in the centre, defined by a meandering wall and surrounded by an arcaded space. Both demonstrate the principle of what are today known as free-running buildings that are not heated or cooled during particular seasons. Instead the interior environment is the result of the interaction of the material and spatial organisation of the building with the local climate. Such examples might point the way towards different and more heterogeneous relations between exterior and interior climate and towards an updated and locally specific sustainable design.

(The architect) must renew architecture from the moment when it was abandoned; and he must try to bridge the existing gap in its development by analysing the elements of change, applying modern techniques to modify the valid methods established by our ancestors, and then developing new solutions that satisfy modern needs.[4]

For architecture to unfold a broad relevance that connects the past and present to the future, Fathy's approach needs to be coupled with what Jeffrey Kipnis termed 'pointing':

Architecture must be projective, ie, it must point to the emergence of new social arrangements and to the construction of new institutional forms. In order to accomplish this, the building must have a point, ie, project a transformation of a prevailing political context.[5]

Altogether the above presents no simple feat: to detect realised and latent potentials in past and present architectures and novel potentials in the way in which rearticulated realised and latent potentials may combine and are actualised in the fast-evolving specific contexts that make up our world today. This clearly ties into questions of cultural identity and context-specific geo-ecological and biophysical processes and the lifestyles related to these.[6]

What, then, constitutes Iranian sensibilities of the past, present and future? What are the past traits that merit rethinking, rearticulating and connecting to relevant contemporary approaches, and what sort of novel amalgamation might point towards promising futures for Iranian architectural design? The work presented in this issue of △ indicates a number of auspicious traits: (1) the past embedded, auxiliary and integrated character of historical architectures that combine spatial, material and formal articulation with its associated multifunctional capacities and link it to the dynamic of local (multi-) cultural and environmental contexts; (2) the past knowledge and skills to put to task the entire scale range of architectural articulation down to the most minute ones for the prior purpose and in an integrated manner that facilitates rather than delimits aesthetic preference specific to locality and time; (3) the past ability to advance architectures in an unprecedented manner whenever different cultural sensibilities are brought together – based on an acute awareness of the time-specific availability of the available scope of knowledge and skills and the projective ability to anticipate what might spring from it (as was the case in Safavid Isfahan with the emergence of projects such as the Khaju Bridge (*pol-e khajoo*) (c 1650) and the music chamber of the Ali Qapu Palace;[7] (4) the past skilful deployment of the building section in the articulation of stunning spaces that produce heterogeneous and comfortable exterior and interior climates;

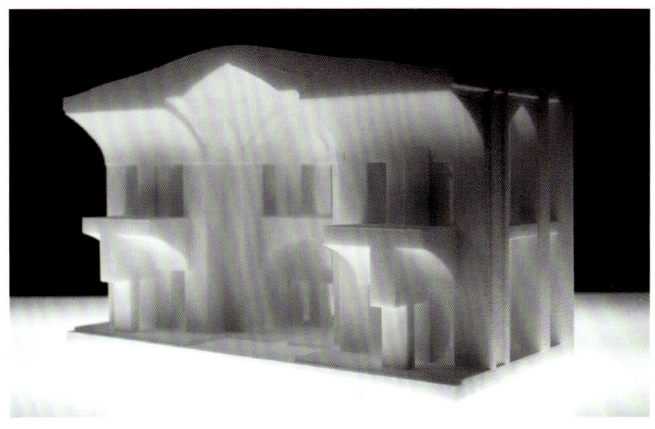

> *While some promising contemporary approaches aim again for an embedded multifunctionality, the vast majority of approaches simply produce a pseudo-historical pastiche in response to an increasing cultural nostalgia, as can be seen, for example, in Neo-Ottoman architectures.*

and (5) the propensity of present architectures to deploy the building section and envelope as a primary device for design innovation, with the former tending to extend the threshold between surroundings and interior by way of an articulated extended terrain, and the latter spreading the climatic threshold into a heterogeneous field.

In general these traits may well apply to a whole host of non-Iranian architectures. The question is, then, what is the pivotal factor that makes architectures determinedly Iranian?

Is the pivotal factor the choice of formal expression and ornamentation? Certainly this is of importance; yet, as has been shown in the article 'Towards an Architectural History of Performance: Auxiliarity, Performance and Provision in Historical Persian Architectures' (pp 26–37), such expression and multifunctional capacity were once inseparably connected. In turn it is of interest to compare the past and present role of formal expression and ornamentation. While some promising contemporary approaches aim again for an embedded multifunctionality, the vast majority of approaches simply produce a pseudo-historical pastiche in response to an increasing cultural nostalgia, as can be seen, for example, in Neo-Ottoman architectures. Should this be dismissed? Perhaps not, as it would seem that such nostalgia may be driven by the longing for forms of expression that generate a sense of cultural identity in the onslaught of the global generic. Yet the production of pseudo-historical pastiche lacks the element of 'pointing' and often reinforces conservative trends instead. The predicament lies in the fact that there is profit to be made in the context of an accelerated increase of such pastiche, and current trends in architecture that are thought to be novel in their approach to form, pattern and ornamentation fall into the trap of actually reinforcing conservatism instead of being pointing, no matter what technological innovation may be involved. Such developments are therefore not simply counteracted by the introduction of new materials or material systems that deliver a contemporary look to the historical reference. Different approaches to this problem are urgently needed.

So is the pivotal factor simply the geographic location? As almost everywhere else in the developed world, the vast majority of contemporary architecture in Iran is entirely nondescript in that it bears no specific relation to context. There must thus be a much greater specificity involved in what constitutes location. This involves the climate, geo-ecological and biophysical processes that are locally specific. Neighbouring regions share Iran's mainly hot arid and cold semi-arid climate. They also shared specific traits in past architectures and are equally nondescript today due to electrical–mechanical interior climatisation. If climate is to be decisive in architectural design it would be necessary to re-instigate what are today called 'free-running' buildings that modulate the interior environment by way of the physical

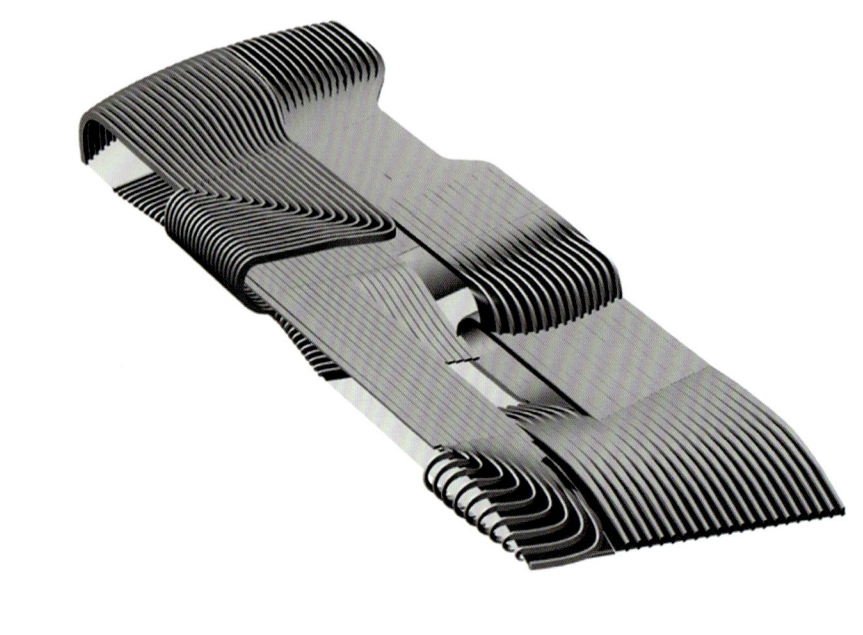

As almost everywhere else in the developed world, the vast majority of contemporary architecture in Iran is entirely nondescript in that it bears no specific relation to context. There must thus be a much greater specificity involved in what constitutes location. This involves the climate, geo-ecological and biophysical processes that are locally specific.

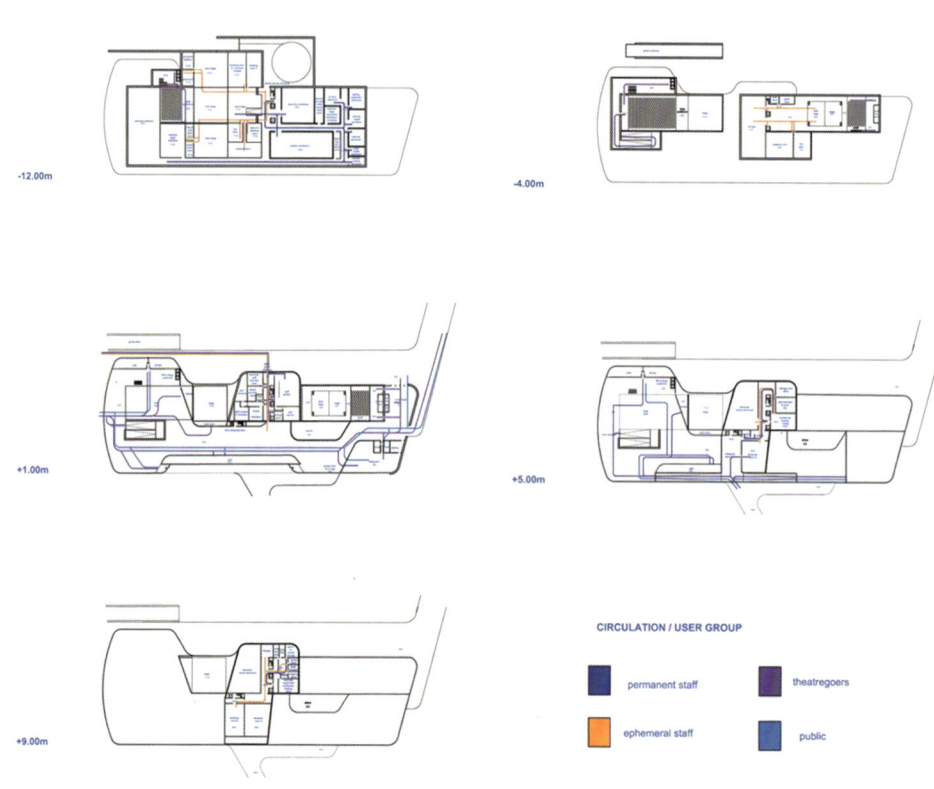

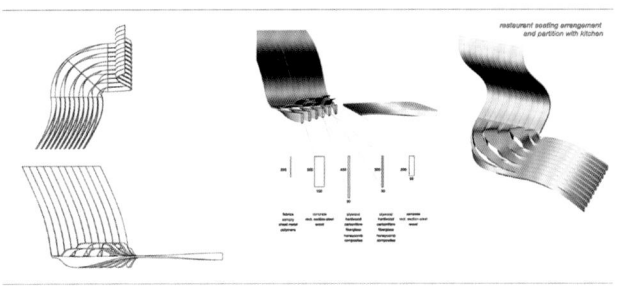
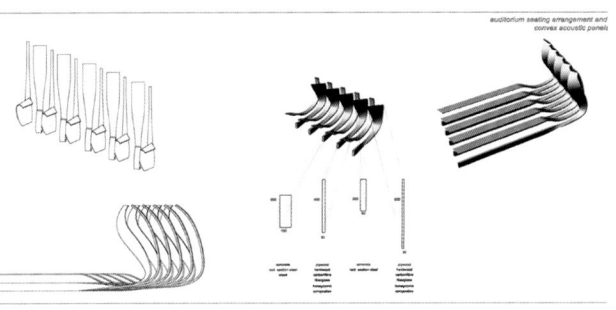
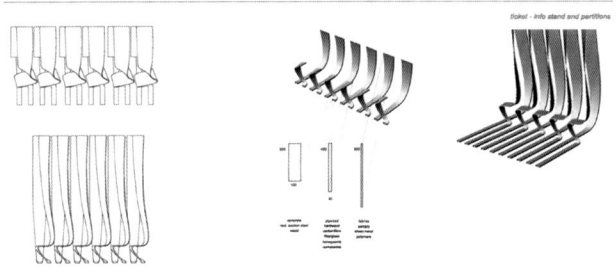

Nasrin Kalbasi and Dimitrios Tsigos, Copenhagen Playhouse Competition, AA Diploma Unit 4 (Michael Hensel and Ludo Grooteman), Architectural Association (AA), London, 2001–2
The playhouse features an articulated envelope and an extended threshold between exterior and interior. The project rearticulates Bahram Shirdel's experiments in striated tectonics into a scheme that combines convergence and divergence of striated elements into continuous and discontinuous surface areas, which regulate movement and provide views across the site and throughout.

opposite top: Aerial view of the scheme and its articulation as a tectonic landscape.

opposite bottom: Plan organisation of spaces arising out of the landform of the project.

bottom and opposite centre: Rendered views of the striated tectonic landscape.

left: Size transitions of the striated envelope that articulate, in a seamless manner, the tectonic landscape of the project and the human dimensions, related provisions and furnishings of the extended landform.

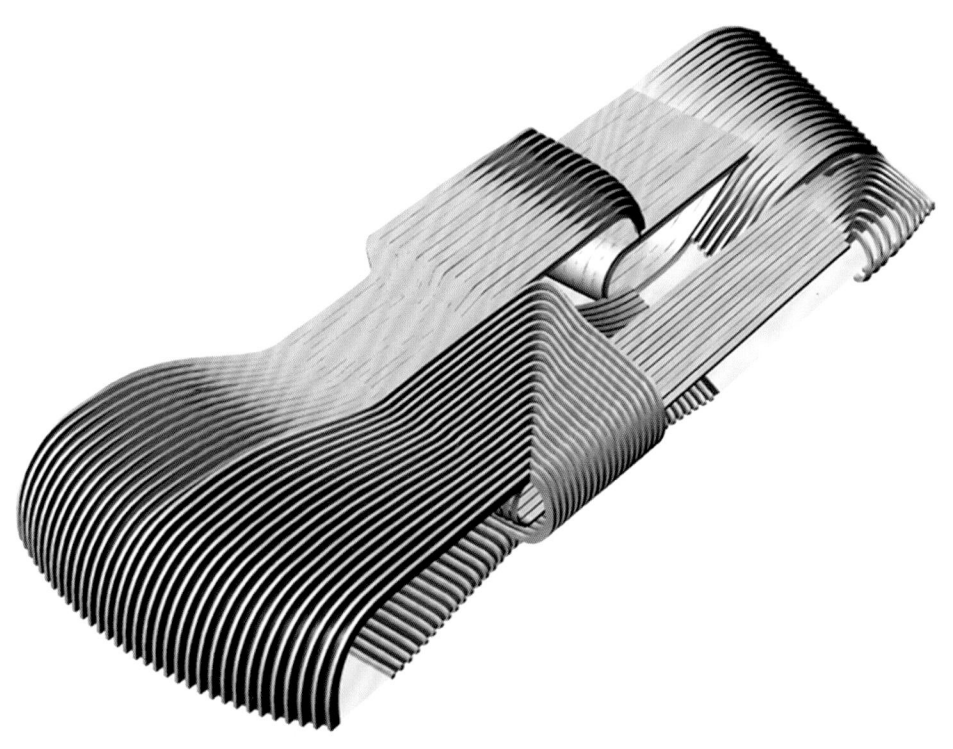

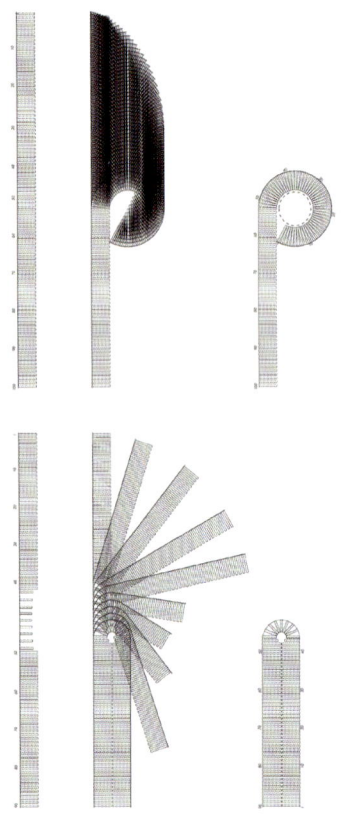

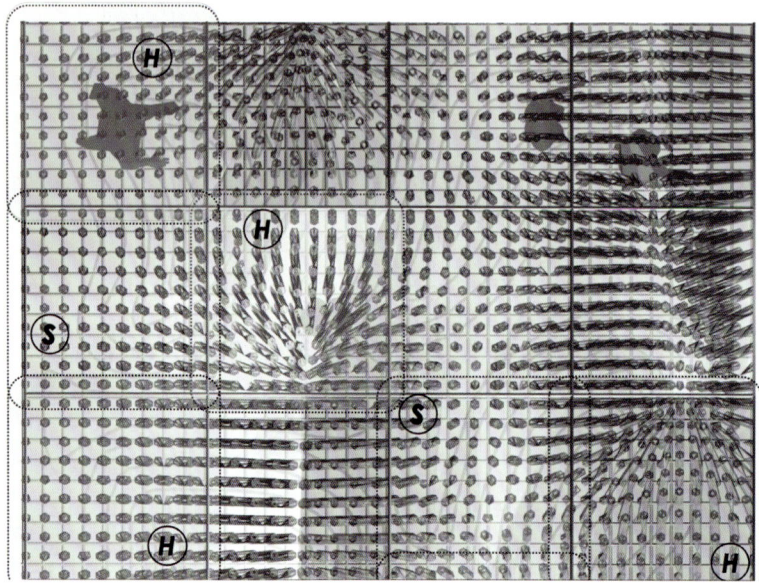

If qanats provided an effective way to irrigate gardens, for example, they may well contribute to the emergence of a type of landscape urbanism that is specific to arid and semi-arid regions with the geological conditions that facilitate the implementation of such systems.

articulation of the building instead of by way of added technology all year round. If new thoughts such as accounting for the adaptive capacity of humans in relation to interior climate variation[8] can be coupled with the heterogeneous provisions of historical architectures, we might be on track to a versatile approach. This may entail that some portion of an architecture is considered in terms of a relatively constant interior environment that gradually adjusts to seasonal differences, while a larger portion provides a heterogeneous climate that offers choice. The architectures in the articles 'Towards an Architectural History of Performance: Auxiliarity, Performance and Provision in Historical Persian Architectures' and 'Persian Gardens and Landscapes' (pp 26–37 and 38–51) might suggest a way forward.

Moreover, dealing with climate and geological conditions raises questions of auxiliarity, for example regarding relations to the local water regime. The subterranean water system of the qanats and its diffusion to regions with very similar conditions shows a way in which multiple new types of architectures emerged and existing architectures could benefit by being linked to such systems. Interesting questions arise from this. If qanats provided an effective way to irrigate gardens, for example, they may well contribute to the emergence of a type of landscape urbanism that is specific to arid and semi-arid regions with the geological conditions that facilitate the implementation of such systems. The interlinking of such

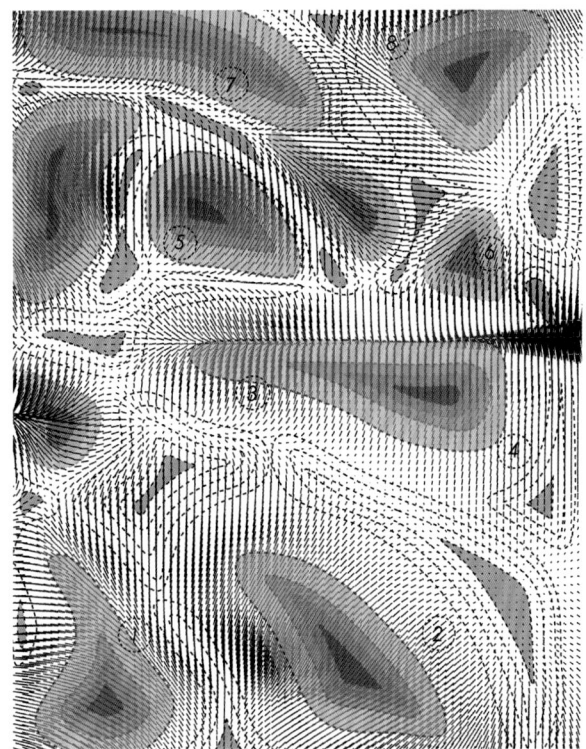

Nazaneen Roxanne Shafaie, Articulated Envelope Experiments, AA Diploma Unit 4 (Michael Hensel and Achim Menges), Architectural Association (AA), London, 2003–4
This research by design experiment explored concepts of material performance, the active architectural boundary and articulated envelope that engages the local climate in the production of a heterogeneous microclimate. In so doing it rearticulated the multifunctional traditional Islamic screen-wall as a thickened system that provides for light, thermal and airflow modulation and view regulation. Due to its depth the system can be used in multiple orientations from vertical to horizontal.

opposite left: The material system consists of a flexible lattice and timber bars positioned normal to the lattice.

opposite right and page 120: Axonometric view and plan of a selected portion of the screen.

left: Map showing an overlay of the timber element orientation and resulting sunlight intensity on the floor surface beneath the screen at midday on 21 June.

ancient systems with contemporary urban conditions and systems does not indicate a nostalgic conservative trend, but instead the emergence of highly interrelated new types of architectures and urban fabric.

Perhaps in the future there might exist two kinds of Iranian architecture: one located in the Iranian cultural and environmental context that springs from past and present local accomplishments and that is re-articulated in a forward-looking innovative manner, and another that is adapted to different contexts. The former may initially be easier to picture, while the latter brings with it further interesting questions such as how a context-specifically adapted Iranian sensibility might be different from a Turkish, Tibetan or Tanzanian one. The development of both the updated context-specific and the context-adapted Iranian sensibilities will rely on how prepared Iranian architects are to do the hard and often underpaid work that is necessary to get there. As it would seem, quite a few appear to be keen and capable. If they have the stamina to be in there for the long run we shall look forward to the futures of Iranian architecture(s). 1

Notes
1. C Alexander, *Notes on the Synthesis of Form*, Harvard University Press (Cambridge, MA), 1964, pp 4–5.
2. P Ricoeur, *Universal Civilisation and National Cultures: History and Truth*, North Western University Press (Evanston, IL), 1965, pp 276–7, and K Frampton, 'Towards a Critical Regionalism: Six Points for an Architecture of Resistance', in H Foster (ed), *The Anti-Aesthetic: Essays on Postmodern Culture*, Bay Press (Port Townsend, WA), 1983, pp 16–30.
3. Frampton, op cit.
4. H Fathy, *Natural Energy and Vernacular Architecture: Principles and Examples with Reference to Hot Arid Climates*, University of Chicago Press (Chicago, IL), 1986, p. xxiii.
5. J Kipnis, 'Towards a New Architecture', in Greg Lynn, *Folding in Architecture* 63(3–4), 1993, pp 40–9.
6. P Reitan, 'Sustainability Science – and What's Needed Beyond Science', *Sustainability: Science, Practice, & Policy* 1(1), 2005, pp 77–80. Online at: http://sspp.proquest.com/archives/vol1iss1/communityessay.reitan.pdf.
7. Multicultural conditions are far from being an exclusively contemporary condition. It seems odd that politicians today can declare the failure of the 'multicultural project' in the face of the fact that in historical times immense accomplishments have arisen out of the close local interaction between peoples of different cultural backgrounds whenever suitable conditions were provided. The question may, then, focus on whether the way the multicultural project today is provided for is adequate, in that it may either make possible or prevent the specific cultures cross-informing one another in a particular way instead of adhering to the globally generic.
8. RJ de Dear and GS Brager, 'Towards an Adaptive Model of Thermal Comfort and Preference', *ASHRAE Transactions* 104(1), 1998, pp 145–67.

Text © 2012 John Wiley & Sons Ltd.
Images © Michael Hensel

COUNTERPOINT

Farrokh Derakhshani

IRAN IN THE REGIONAL CONTEXT

For much of its history, Iran was part of an extensive empire with far-reaching trade and cultural networks. The current political situation, however, has often led to a misplaced patriotism that has emphasised the heritage of the nation state over its connections across the region. **Farrokh Derakhshani** flags up the danger of appropriating a wider common heritage from a local rather than a global perspective, and looks at Iran in the wider context of its immediate neighbours.

Hassan Fathy, New Gourna Mosque, near Luxor, Egypt, 1952
New Gourna came to international attention some 20 years after Fathy finished work on it, with the publication of his book *Architecture for the Poor: An Experiment in Rural Egypt* (1973). New Gourna was built in order to relocate the villagers of old Gourna, who were living off the looting of antiquities, away from the site of the Valley of the Kings. Despite Fathy's thoughtful design of individual dwelling and enlightened consideration of natural ventilation, orientation, energy conservation and local building techniques, which were all ahead of their time, the project was not wholly successful – the resettlement was imposed on the villagers by the government. The mosque with its distinct staircase minaret is now one of the few existing structures on this World Heritage site.

In the search for a better understanding of the architecture of a specific city, country or region, a whole range of approaches can be taken to history, climate, material and social context(s). However, in most cases, it is convenient and expedient to single out a particular building, or even a neighbourhood, and look at it as an isolated object, immortalised in time; glorifying selected buildings or urban fabrics; criticising the current condition through a lens of false nostalgia for an idealised past. A number of articles in this issue of △ eloquently describe architectural history and heritage as a source of inspiration (and sometimes obligation) for designing for the future. But the most exciting aspect of the built environment is its complexity and behaviour in time. What we as architects find truly difficult is to derive inspiration from the life and spirit of this heritage and to understand its meaning and symbolism rather than just the formal aspects. Our buildings are not isolated from our cities, societies and cultural values. Today we feel much more a part of the larger world than our ancestors. As our human context moves further from the local towards the global, our sense of civic responsibility needs to extend beyond our homes, neighbourhoods, communities and cities. It is, therefore, the architecture and urban spaces we seek to create that represent a material manifestation of our behaviour, and which are the true representation of our societies.

So where are the boundaries of 'Iranian architecture' and how is it different to the 'architecture of Iran'? Historically, geographic boundaries, language, faith, race or ethnicity have not been the binding elements of what is considered Iranian; it is culture that defines what is Iranian or Persian;[1] a culture that has been created and shared by many people for thousands of years. From an architectural perspective, architectural vocabulary, building materials and climate are the key elements that have been shaped by a sense of order and concept of space that has emerged from this continuous culture. There are many similarities in the architecture of monuments in Turkestan (on the Chinese border of Kazakhstan), Samarkand and Bukhara (in Uzbekistan) in the east, and the Mogul architecture of northern India, to the domestic and monumental heritage of Caucasus in the Russian Federation and Azerbaijan, tombs and madrasas in Anatolia, shrines and mosques in Iraq and finally souks and urban architectural heritage in Dubai and Doha, with buildings in the Iranian plateau.

The sheer size of the lands and number of peoples that various Iranian dynasties ruled for over 5,000 years also created opportunities to bring together thinkers, builders

OHO Joint Venture (Atelier Frei Otto, Buro Happold, Omrania Architects), Tuwaiq Palace, Riyadh, Saudi Arabia, 1985
Originally designed as a diplomatic club for the international community, the palace has a dramatic promontory site overlooking the valley of Wadi Hanifeh. Drawing on Otto's expertise in tensile structures, it is an imaginative combination of traditional types – bringing together the fortress and the tent – in a beautiful garden, oasis-like setting.

and architects from across the empire to create magnificent structures, demonstrating a global rather than a local approach to architecture. In building Persepolis in the 6th century BC, wood was brought from Lebanon and India and stone carvers from Greece. During times of weak central governments, builders and artists would migrate to neighbouring empires and offer their architectural knowhow and services. Today, because of political conditions and nationalistic attitudes, there is a desire to appropriate this common heritage as a source of pride from a local rather than a global perspective.[2]

Since the late 19th century, the long-established processes of shaping the built environment have changed along with other aspects of life in Iran. The country has moved from a traditional society to a modern state, like most countries in the region, especially Turkey and Egypt. They have been moving forward on parallel tracks towards 'modernisation', each at its own speed depending on the political, economic and social reality of its recent history. I prefer the term 'modernisation' rather than 'Westernisation', which is used by many scholars, as people from many continents were active contributors to this process of thinking, and this thrust of ideas did not necessarily always flow from West to East or from North to South. The speed of change accelerated between the two World Wars with more exchanges and interactions between the different parts of the world. In terms of building and urban interventions, this can be seen in the introduction of stylistic movements of the time, from Neoclassicism, Modernism, contextual architecture, and so on. The cities of Alexandria, Cairo, Baghdad and Beirut at the beginning of the 20th century were competing with European cities of the epoque in introducing a modern lifestyle and modern buildings. These were places of experimentation and laboratories for new ideas in architecture and urban design. Foreign architects, building in all of these cities, which at the time were at their peak, were translating the aspirations of local people or implementing the colonial will of the ruling power.

New developments in the construction industry and progress in building technology that spread around the globe were major elements in globalising the built environment. Villas of the 1950s, inspired by American and European architecture, could be seen in the affluent neighbourhoods of Beirut, Alexandria, Istanbul and Tehran. Banks, hospitals, office and apartment buildings followed the same patterns. The Istanbul Hilton by Skidmore, Owings & Merrill (SOM) and Sedad Hakki Eldem, built in 1955, and the Tehran Royal Hilton by Ghiai, Sadegh & Foroughi, built in 1962, set new 'modern' standards in public buildings.

The similarities in creativity in these countries can also be seen in other disciplines such as literature, art and film. For example, Iranian, Egyptian and Turkish Neo-realist films of the

Kamran Diba, Tehran Museum of Contemporary Art, Tehran, 1977
above: With its idiosyncratic extrusions – influenced by Iranian wind towers – the museum fuses the traditional with the modern. It was designed and founded by artist and architect Kamran Diba as a series of interconnected galleries spiralling downwards underground.

1950s project a similar vision for urban life and modern living.

The 1950s onwards saw a parallel attempt among the intelligentsia in search of the 'local modern', and in architecture this was not only expressed in formal aspects in the design of buildings, but also in architectural discourse. In Turkey, Sedad Hakki Eldem (1926–86) was a pioneer; his ideas and buildings have had a great impact on the next generation of architects. In Egypt, Hassan Fathy introduced the idea of 'architecture for the poor', which was welcomed internationally before being accepted by Egyptian architects.[3] Rifat Chadirji's projects in the 1960s and 1970s, and his writing in Arabic, reached far beyond his home country Iraq. Iran in the late 1960s and early 1970s enjoyed a blooming of a contemporary Iranian architecture by a number of young architects. In 1978, Bernard Huet, editor of *l'Architecture d'aujourd'hui*, dedicated an issue to Hassan Fathy and the new Iranian architecture, introducing these emerging trends to a Western audience.

In the 1980s and 1990s, following the oil boom and the introduction of free-market policies, some countries (including Turkey, and especially in the Gulf region) witnessed a construction boom. In Iran, the 1979 revolution, eight years of war with Iraq, a Western boycott and mass migration of the intelligentsia caused a rupture of architectural production. Although a large quantity of construction took place, the

Skidmore Owings & Merrill (SOM) and Sedad Hakki Eldem, Istanbul Hilton, Istanbul, 1955
opposite right: Turkey's first five-star hotel with 258 rooms, the Istanbul Hilton epitomised the modern. Corbusian in style, it was raised on concrete pilotis, with box-like balconies, and had a domed nightclub.

Rifat Chadirji, Etchings of Federation of Iraqi Industries, Baghdad, 1966
below: Chadirji's search for a regional Modernism that synthesised elements of the rich Islamic heritage with the principles of 20th-century international architecture, found expression in cement-concrete buildings and in his plans for Baghdad.

New developments in the construction industry and progress in building technology that spread around the globe were major elements in globalising the built environment. Villas of the 1950s, inspired by American and European architecture, could be seen in the affluent neighbourhoods of Beirut, Alexandria, Istanbul and Tehran.

131

quality of the work was questionable. Architects who remained in the country were confronted with new challenges and demands to create, mostly for public projects, an architecture that represented the 'true' Islamic identity of Iran.

On one hand, Iran's politics in the last 30 years have isolated the country from the Western world, resulting in less commercial, academic and touristic exchange; on the other hand, for the first time in Iran's history, an important number of its population have migrated around the globe. The connection between this diaspora with their families and friends back home has created a widespread interaction with the world that did not exist in the country prior to the revolution. From a population of 50 million in 1979, only some 200,000 lived abroad at the time: today that number is more than 3 million. Although satellite TV and foreign media are forbidden in the country, thanks to the Internet and the growing number of media-savvy, educated youth Iranian society is aware of, and well versed in, global movements of ideas. While symbols of globalisation are not to be seen in Iranian cities – there are no international hotel chains, McDonald's or Starbucks, and most multinational corporations (IBM, Microsoft) are absent due to the US boycott – there are local versions of everything, even in the most remote small cities.

Iranian people, as clients and users of architecture, compare themselves to Turkey and the UAE, their two immediate neighbours (which they visit most), which are marked by two different approaches to architectural production. In Turkey, the economic boom, professional capacity in the construction sector and large number of universities has created a local knowledge that is exported internationally. In Dubai and other Gulf states the ambitious building boom is dominated by foreign designers and builders, and in some cases used mainly by foreigners.

Foreign architects and construction companies do not build in Iran (except for a few recent exceptions) and the lack of vision and constraints on public projects rarely give architects the freedom to explore and express their creativity. The struggle between a search for a new imagined identity and ruthless market forces has made the urbanscape characterless in most Iranian cities. One of the only areas in which high standards have been achieved in the last two decades is restoration and conservation. However, today there is new hope for a new architecture in Iran. A younger generation of Iranian architects are producing better designs, especially for the private sector. Established architects have been given the opportunity to build new diplomatic buildings in many capitals of the world as part of an ambitious governmental programme to change the image of Iran abroad. (See pp 86–7, for instance, for Hadi

Tabanlıoğlu Architects, Doğan Media Center, Ankara, Turkey, 2008
Built to house both the TV channels and newspaper of one of Turkey's principal media groups, the architects aimed to express the openness of communication through a transparent mass, punctuated by perforated aluminium panels on the facade – 'an updated traditional latticework screen'.

Tens of thousands of architectural students in Iran are looking for good models and sources of inspiration to be able to build a better tomorrow. Appropriate influences and built examples are already within their reach. They need only to understand the right balance between their own vision and the means of realising it before starting to take responsibility for the future.

Mirmiran's General Consulate of Iran in Frankfurt, 2004.) Iranian architects and construction professionals do hope that one day they can take advantage of the building boom in neighbouring countries to expand their horizons and engage in a broader discourse with talent from around the world. Tens of thousands of architectural students in Iran are looking for good models and sources of inspiration to be able to build a better tomorrow. Appropriate influences and built examples are already within their reach. They need only to understand the right balance between their own vision and the means of realising it before starting to take responsibility for the future. 𐐑

Notes
1. Since the early 20th century there has been confusion in the European languages between 'Persia' and 'Iran' or 'Persian' and 'Iranian', which are the same concept in the original language.
2. In 2009, eight countries requested the inclusion of Nowruz (the Iranian New Year) on UNESCO's Intangible Cultural Heritage List.
3. Hassan Fathy, *Architecture for the Poor: An Experiment in Rural Egypt*, University of Chicago Press (Chicago, IL), 1973.

Abdel-Halim Community Development Collaborative and Sasaki and Associates, American University in Cairo Campus, Cairo, 2008
This collaboration between an Egyptian and a US practice fuses the tradition of American liberal arts campuses with a more local Islamic design tradition; the architectural harmony is drawn from the geometry, materials and landscaping.

Architecture by Collective Terrain (AbCT)/ Ramin Mehdizadeh, Apartment No 1, Mahallat, Iran, 2010
Built in a small town in central Iran, where stone-cutting is one of the main industries, this apartment block connects to its context by using locally recycled stones. The stone is set on the facade at emphatic angles to expressive affect, giving it a sharp modern elevation.

Text © 2012 John Wiley & Sons Ltd. Images: p 128(t) © Christopher Little/Aga Khan Trust for Culture; pp 128(b), 130 © Aga Khan Trust for Culture; p 129 © Courtesy of Omrania/Aga Khan Trust for Culture; p 131 © Courtesy of Rifat Chadirji/ Aga Khan Trust for Culture; p 132 © Cemal Emden/Aga Khan Trust for Culture; p 133 © Barry Iverson/Aga Khan Trust for Culture; p 134 © Omid Khodapanahi/Aga Khan Trust for Culture

CONTRIBUTORS

Salmaan Craig studied industrial design before undertaking an engineering doctorate on the thermal physics of building envelopes, in collaboration with Brunel University and Buro Happold. His interest in Persian ice-makers stems from this period when he began to explore ways of utilising night-sky radiative cooling. He now works in the Specialist Modelling Group at Foster + Partners.

Reza Daneshmir and **Catherine Spiridinoff** established **Fluid Motion Architects** (FMA) in Tehran in 2004 and in 2008 added the R&D department, named iRODE. To date the studio has designed and overseen a number of different architectural and urban design projects. The study of dynamic and flowing structures and forms is part of its key conceptual approaches, including the integration of spaces and structures to create an open dialogue between the metropolis and important architectural elements, and to develop architectural places that become new points of attraction within a city. In 2009 the practice's Mellat Park Cineplex was shortlisted in the culture category of the World Architecture Festival.

Farrokh Derakhshani is Director of the Aga Khan Award for Architecture and has been associated with the award since 1982. His main field of specialisation is the contemporary architecture of Muslim societies. He lectures widely, and has organised and participated in numerous international seminars, exhibitions, colloquia, workshops and competitions. He has served as a jury member at various international competitions and schools of architecture and collaborated on a large variety of publications on architecture. He trained as an architect and planner at the National University of Iran and later continued his studies at the School of Architecture in Paris (UP1).

Darab Diba is a professor of architecture at Tehran University and the Azad Islamic University, and was a director of the PhD programme of architecture at Tehran University from 1995 to 2003. He is a guest professor at MIT-Harvard, the École d'Architecture Paris-Belleville, and the École Polytechnique Fédérale de Lausanne (EPFL) School of Architecture. He has been Editor & Director of *Architecture & Urbanism* since 2000, and was on the Master Jury of the Aga Khan Award for Architecture from 1998 to 2001. His countries of expertise include Indonesia, Malaysia, Bangladesh, Morocco, India, Pakistan, Syria, Lebanon, Dubai and Iran. He is a principal at ATEC Consultants, Architects, Engineers & Urban Planners, a member of the board and committee director of architectural design. He received the National Prize of Architecture from the Ministry of Housing and Urban Development, Tehran, in 2000, and the United Nations Special Award (UN Habitat) in 2011. Fields of research include world contemporary architecture and the contemporary architecture of Islamic countries, new comparative theories and expressions of architecture in emergent countries, and the relationship of art, architecture, environment and context.

Nasrine Faghih is an Iranian-born architect currently practising in Iran and France. Her built work has covered a broad range of typologies including residential housing, cultural and civic spaces, Islamic gardens and masterplanning. She was the Me'mar prizewinner in 2009. She has taught in both Europe and America, and has published internationally, including several articles on Iranian and Islamic gardens and, most recently, *Conversation with a Young Architect* (Research Center Publisher, 2009) and *Zero Carbon Cities* (Rahshahr International Group, 2009). She is the president of Boostan International Solidarity, a founding member of the Aga Khan Award for Architecture, and an Individual Expert for the European Community in Infrastructure. She earned her doctorate in architecture from the Istituto Universitario di Architettura in Venice, and her Master of Environmental Design from Yale University in 1973.

Farshad Farahi is an Iranian architect, practitioner and scholar who co-founded Naqsh-e-Jahan-Pars (NJP) consulting engineers and collaborated with Bahram Shirdel in Iran. During his career he has contributed to many award-winning projects and been a guest lecturer and visiting professor. He was an editorial board member of the Iranian *A&U* magazine, and has authored articles on Iranian art and architecture. He received his masters degree in architecture from the National University of Iran, and continued his education at the San Francisco Art Institute and University of Southern California. He currently lives and practises in the Washington DC area.

Amin Sadeghy received his Bachelor of Architecture from Tehran University of Science and Technology. In 2007 he went to London where he studied at the Architectural Association (AA) and received his Master of Science in Emergent Technologies and Design. He is an architect and researcher, and has been working for Foster + Partners since 2008, where he has been involved with the Masdar Zero Carbon City in Abu Dhabi and an enormous campus office project in the US. In 2009 he co-founded studio INTEGRATE with Mehran Gharleghi, which has won several design awards. He lectured at the House of Architecture in Graz in 2011, and the AA Fab Research Cluster Symposium in London in 2009, and his work was presented at the Acadia 2009 and Smart Geometry 2009 conferences. He has been a jury member at the AA, UEL and Metropolitan University. studio INTEGRATE exhibited its Responsive Pneumatic Systems research at London's Design Festival in 2009.

Saman Sayar was born in Tehran. He studied architecture at the Islamic Azad University of Qazvin (1996–2004) where he obtained his MArch. He worked from 1998 to 2004 with the architect Hadi Mirmiran on different architectural and urban design projects and competitions. Since 2004 he has continued working at Naqsh-e-Jahan-Pars (NJP) consulting engineers as project architect and coordinator. He also teaches architecture at the Islamic Azad University of Qazvin.

Defne Sunguroğlu Hensel is an architect, interior architect and researcher. She is a founding member and vice-chair of the OCEAN Design Research Association, and founding and board member of the international Sustainable Environment Association (SEA), both registered in Norway. She is a research fellow at the Oslo School of Architecture and Design where she is pursuing her PhD on 'Multiple Performance Integration Models Based on Wood- and Clay-Based Systems'.

ABOUT ARCHITECTURAL DESIGN

INDIVIDUAL BACKLIST ISSUES OF △ ARE AVAILABLE FOR PURCHASE AT £22.99 / US$45

TO ORDER AND SUBSCRIBE SEE BELOW

What is *Architectural Design*?

Founded in 1930, *Architectural Design* (△) is an influential and prestigious publication. It combines the currency and topicality of a newsstand journal with the rigour and production qualities of a book. With an almost unrivalled reputation worldwide, it is consistently at the forefront of cultural thought and design.

Each title of △ is edited by an invited guest-editor, who is an international expert in the field. Renowned for being at the leading edge of design and new technologies, △ also covers themes as diverse as: architectural history, the environment, interior design, landscape architecture and urban design.

Provocative and inspirational, △ inspires theoretical, creative and technological advances. It questions the outcome of technical innovations as well as the far-reaching social, cultural and environmental challenges that present themselves today.

For further information on △, subscriptions and purchasing single issues see: www.architectural-design-magazine.com

How to Subscribe

With 6 issues a year, you can subscribe to △ (either print or online), or buy titles individually.

Subscribe today to receive 6 issues delivered direct to your door!

INSTITUTIONAL SUBSCRIPTION
£230 / US$431 combined print & online

INSTITUTIONAL SUBSCRIPTION
£200 / US$375 print or online

PERSONAL RATE SUBSCRIPTION
£120 / US$189 print only

STUDENT RATE SUBSCRIPTION
£75 / US$117 print only

To subscribe:
Tel: +44 (0) 1243 843272
Email: cs-journals@wiley.com

Volume 81 No 1
ISBN 978 04707 47209

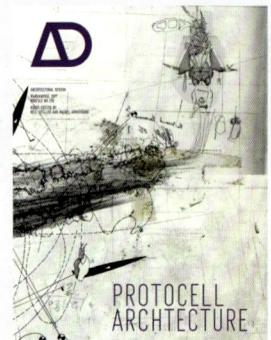

Volume 81 No 2
ISBN 978 0470 748282

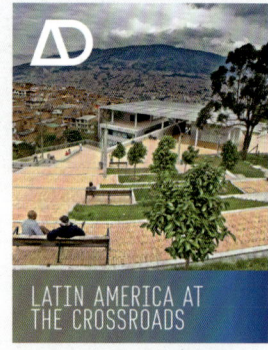

Volume 81 No 3
ISBN 978 0470 664926

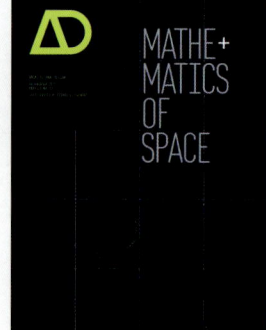

Volume 81 No 4
ISBN 978 0470 686806

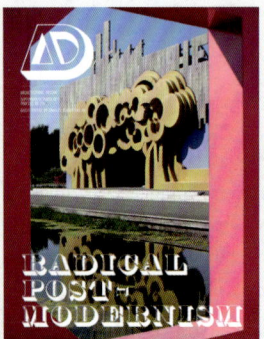

Volume 81 No 5
ISBN 978 0470 669884

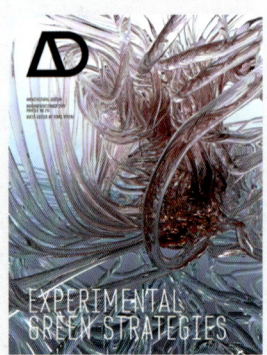

Volume 81 No 6
ISBN 978 0470 689790

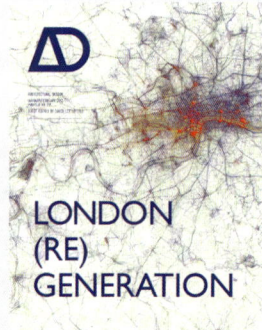

Volume 82 No 1
ISBN 978 1119 993780

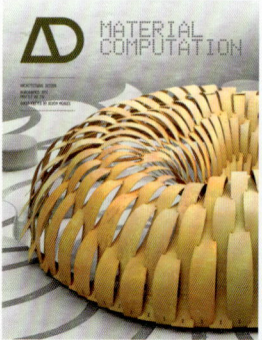

Volume 82 No 2
ISBN 978 0470 973301